The Girl from the
Fiction Department

Sonia

10.7.65.

The Girl from the Fiction Department

A Portrait of Sonia Orwell

HILARY SPURLING

HAMISH HAMILTON
an imprint of
PENGUIN BOOKS

HAMISH HAMILTON LTD

Published by the Penguin Group
Penguin Books Ltd, 80 Strand, London WC2R ORL, England
Penguin Putnam Inc., 375 Hudson Street, New York, New York 10014, USA
Penguin Books Australia Ltd, 250 Camberwell Road,
Camberwell, Victoria 3124, Australia
Penguin Books Canada Ltd, 10 Alcorn Avenue, Toronto, Ontario, Canada M4V 3B2
Penguin Books India (P) Ltd, 11 Community Centre,
Panchsheel Park, New Delhi – 110 017, India
Penguin Books (NZ) Ltd, Cnr Rosedale and Airborne Roads,
Albany, Auckland, New Zealand
Penguin Books (South Africa) (Pty) Ltd, 24 Sturdee Avenue,
Rosebank 2196, South Africa

Penguin Books Ltd, Registered Offices: 80 Strand, London WC2R ORL, England

On the World Wide Web at: www.penguin.com

First published 2002
1

Set in 12/14.25 pt Monotype Dante
Typeset by Rowland Phototypesetting Ltd, Bury St Edmunds, Suffolk
Printed in Great Britain by Clays Ltd, St Ives plc

A CIP catalogue record for this book is available from the British Library

ISBN 0 – 241 – 14165 – 6

FRONTISPIECE: Picasso's dedication to Sonia from *Les Dames de Mougins*.

For Amy

'the girl from the Fiction Department . . . was looking at him . . . She was very young, he thought, she still expected something from life . . . She would not accept it as a law of nature that the individual is always defeated . . . All you needed was luck and cunning and boldness. She did not understand that there was no such thing as happiness, that the only victory lay in the far future, long after you were dead.'

George Orwell, *Nineteen Eighty-Four*

Preface

People always made up stories about Sonia. She was dazzling as a girl when she first met George Orwell, and she still could be in her fifties when I knew her. Like countless other friends, I loved her for her gaiety, her generosity and her radiant vitality. She had great power and presence, shadowed by the ominous sense she gave to all who knew her of being haunted or possessed by demons. The French writer Michel Leiris, Sonia's friend for nearly forty years, came to see her as an Arthurian enchantress, a modern equivalent of Morgan le Fay or la Belle Viviane, fearsome beauties whose shadowy presence still lingers faintly on the air at Arthur's Cornish castle of Tintagel, by Dozmary pool on Bodmin Moor, in the legendary forest of Brocéliande, all the ancient Celtic sites – some derelict, some overrun by tourists – that Sonia visited with Leiris on motoring trips to Cornwall, Brittany and Ireland in the last years of her life.

Catastrophe caught up with her at this point. For reasons none of her friends could understand, Sonia dropped out of their lives, explaining nothing, confiding in no one, retreating into a limbo of foreboding and despair. She said she no longer had a future. Books became her sole companions. 'But when I put them down, or when I wake up, it's all there again,' she wrote to a friend in 1979: 'this terrible endless tunnel into which I've drifted which, naturally, I feel is somehow all my fault but from which I'll never emerge again, but worse [I feel] that I've damaged George.' Twelve months later she was dead.

The attacks that began almost at once came as a shock to friends still struggling, like me, to accept what had happened, and unable to comprehend why. Sonia's former ally, Mary McCarthy, trenchantly summed up her weakest points for the memorial gathering. A much younger friend, David Plante, did the same at greater length in *Difficult Women* a few years later. Both accounts were accurate as far as they went, but they left out Sonia's extraordinary warmth, her radiance, her passionate altruism. She was depicted as heartless, greedy and manipulative in *Orwell. The Authorised Biography* by Michael Shelden, whose view of her was widely disputed after the book came out in 1991. The same accusations were repeated in harsher terms ten years later in Jeffrey Meyers's *Orwell. Wintry Conscience of a Generation.*

The myth of the cold and grasping Widow Orwell, based on ignorance, misconception and distortion, had by this time acquired its own momentum. The real Sonia seemed to have been taken over by the fiction department. This book is an attempt to disentangle the truth before she disappears completely. I have tried to pare back what Michael Holroyd called history's cuticle of lies by confronting the central mystery of Sonia's life, the relationship that drove her to her death and that has puzzled people ever since: her role as wife, widow and sole heir to George Orwell.

Hilary Spurling
Paris, November 2001

PART ONE

The First Drop of the Monsoon

*Sonia and her older sister Bay as bridemaids at their mother's
second wedding*

She was born Sonia Brownell at Ranchi in the province of Bihar in India on 25 August 1918, towards the end of the rainy season. One of the few childhood memories she cared to talk about afterwards was the gathering tension of the dry months in India, when the whole world – scorched earth, parched animals, torpid human beings – waited for the first raindrop to fall with an almost inaudible plop, followed by a brisk patter, then the drenching storms and torrential floods of the monsoon: 'and suddenly people could start to live again.'

Sonia's birthplace at Ranchi was in the hills, where her mother had taken refuge from the heat of the Bengal plain. Her father, Charles Brownell, was a freight-broker in the great merchant city of imperial Calcutta. She spent her first five years in Calcutta, and seldom spoke about them afterwards. As an adult, she went back only once, on a leisurely honeymoon voyage with her second husband which took them in 1959 through the still largely unravaged countryside of Thailand, Cambodia, Laos and Vietnam, then back across the subcontinent to Bengal. 'India at last,' she wrote to Michel Leiris from Calcutta: 'all at once it makes the countries of south-east Asia seem like childish make-believe, a Rousseauesque artificial paradise. Here life is real and hard and sad.'

If life was ever anything else for Sonia, it didn't last.

Charles Brownell was an Englishman who had come out in his twenties to seek his fortune in Calcutta, where he found work with Turner, Morrison & Co. and married Beatrice Binning, the youngest of four high-spirited and strong-minded sisters in a large, closely knit, Roman Catholic, Anglo-Indian family. They were a handsome couple. Neither of their fathers had the means to set them up in style, but they made up for want of funds in confidence and dash. Charles, who cut a fine figure on a horse, was secretary of the Tollygunge Gymkhana Race Club. Beatrice was a keen sportswoman, playing golf and tennis to championship standard. She was lively, popular, outward-going, with a sunny temperament and glorious golden hair. Sonia's looks, her generosity, her abundant energy and practicality, her gift for making and keeping friends, all came from her mother.

Sonia was just four months old when Charles Brownell died suddenly on 29 December 1918. He was thirty-six years old. His elder daughter Bay (short for Beatrice), aged four, remembered being kissed goodnight by her father at bedtime, and being woken by screams next morning to learn that he had died on the golf-course in the night. They told her he had had a heart attack. The official burial record gives no cause of death, saying instead that he was buried by a police order which suggests a possible suicide. There were hints of trouble: the loss of his job, unmanageable dressmakers' bills run up by his exuberant young wife. Perhaps he faced ruin, or perhaps he suspected – as Sonia herself would do long afterwards – that the new baby was not in fact his daughter after all. The most that can be said for sure is that, if he had killed himself in the closely

Beatrice Brownell receiving her trophy in the
All India Golf Competition
Charles Brownell on horseback at Calcutta races
Sonia's maternal grandparents, Colonel and Mrs Joseph Binning,
with their six children: Beatrice is the youngest, perched on the
fence next to her mother

regulated, morally prescriptive, socially cohesive world of British India in those days, it would have been hushed up.

Both sisters were marked for ever by that early calamity. Bay, who had dearly loved her father, found it almost

Charles Brownell

impossible to absorb the shock of his loss. Sonia, encountering the outside world for the first time as a fractured household of confused and distracted adults, never fully bonded as a baby with her mother. Plunged into characteristically extravagant mourning, Beatrice acted with equally characteristic decision. Her husband was buried in Calcutta by the Anglican cathedral chaplain on the last day of the year, the baby was baptized a week later by the Roman Catholic priest of St Thomas's church, and the fatherless

family sailed for home, which now meant Charles's Protestant relations in the north of England.

Beatrice promptly succumbed to the epidemic of Spanish
flu that killed more Europeans, in 1918 and the year after,
than the whole of the First World War. She was shut away
with Sonia (who was not yet weaned) to be nursed in
isolation. The four-year-old Bay, apparently abandoned
without warning by both parents, withdrew into a silence
that lasted for twelve months. For many years after that,
she rarely spoke or smiled. Beatrice recovered, and swiftly
solved the problem of survival as a penniless young widow
by taking a highly eligible second husband.

Charming, intelligent, urbane and ten years older than
his future wife, Geoffrey Dixon was a chartered accountant,
newly decorated in 1919 for his contribution to the war
effort, and widely expected to go far. He was already a
director of the firm of Turner, Morrison in Calcutta for
which Brownell had worked as an assistant. Unless the two
met by chance on Geoff Dixon's home leave from India
after the war, he must have known the dashing young Mrs
Brownell as the wife of one of his junior employees in
Calcutta. Perhaps he followed her back to England, where
the couple were married on 5 January 1920, a week to the
day after the end of Beatrice's year of formal widow's
mourning. The wedding took place on the Isle of Wight
with Beatrice's two little daughters as bridesmaids. Bay had
reacted to news of her mother's remarriage by cutting off
all her hair. A wedding photo shows her clutching the hand
of the plump bemused toddler, Sonia, both sisters holding
bouquets and wearing mob caps to hide the fact that the
elder of the two was now bald as well as speechless.

The family returned to Calcutta to settle at number 1 Old Ballygunge Road, a spacious airy house with high ceilings, cool verandahs and a large garden, near the maidan and the parade ground of the Governor General's Bodyguard, at the heart of the fashionable green and leafy district known as Mayfair. A son, Michael, was born in 1921. Sonia adored this little brother who was small enough to boss and boast about, willing enough to follow where she led, bright enough to challenge and stimulate her in return. To the end of her life, she talked of Michael with the fond, proud admiration she had felt for him from birth.

In an active, practical, sporting family, these two were the booky ones, the intellectuals, in some sense the misfits, and in due course the rebels. Forty years on they would speculate about the possibility that they shared the same father. Both felt it made sense of much in their childhood that wasn't otherwise easy to explain. At all events their

Beatrice and her second husband, Geoffrey Dixon

Sonia on stage

similarity in character, and their mutual interests, provided them with an escape hatch when they needed one. It meant they could retreat from tensions at home into a private world of art, literature, ideas, where they could count on the rest of the family to leave them undisturbed.

Their upbringing followed the standard routines of their time and class: picnics, parties, excursions, music, riding and tennis lessons, with ballet for the girls. Bay and Sonia put on cabarets for their parents, dressing up and taking it in turns to sing, dance and recite with the daughter of their mother's best friend, Vivien Hartley (who would grow up to become another great enchantress, the actress Vivien Leigh). Vivien was sent home to an English convent boarding-school on the outskirts of London at the age of six.

Three years later she was joined at the same school by her contemporary, the unhappy and often silent Bay Brownell.

Sonia followed the two bigger girls as soon as she was old enough, starting her first term at the Convent of the Sacred Heart, Roehampton, on 1 September 1924, exactly a week after her sixth birthday. She wrote afterwards about the pathetic survival strategies of children suddenly expelled from home, 'lonely little schemers' learning to be tough by obliterating even the memory of 'the area of their hearts that was turned to stone for ever in the twilight of the first night at school when they lay in bed calculating their new future . . .'

By 1924, or shortly afterwards, things were starting to go wrong for the family in India. Geoff Dixon was drinking hard, becoming increasingly erratic and aggressive, already moving towards the showdown that would cost him his career. Sonia was taken out of her English school after three terms. Over the next two years, her mother's marriage came under mounting strain. Sonia remembered her stepfather veering out of control in bullying rages that sometimes seemed demented. The household cracked apart. Domestic rows erupted into public scandal. In 1927, when Sonia was eight, Geoff Dixon was thrown out of the Calcutta Club and forced to resign from his job, which left him no alternative but to leave India for good.

The family took refuge in Liverpool. Michael fell gravely ill and nearly died of emphysema. Sonia was sent back to board at the Sacred Heart. The situation at home disintegrated until Bay, who had shelved her own problems to become her mother's standby in time of trouble, left school at sixteen in 1930. She persuaded Beatrice to walk out on her abusive alcoholic husband and face what was in those days the appalling stigma of divorce. In a society where the equivalent of political correctness ensured that women of

Beatrice with Sonia, Michael and Bay after the family left India

the middle classes did not work or operate independently, let alone ditch their marriages with impunity, the social penalties were harsher even than the practical problems facing a single mother with three children and no means of support.

From now on the family scraped by on Beatrice's meagre earnings from whatever jobs she could come by without experience or training. She was tough, competent, resource-ful, and a brilliant organizer. She found work as a manager in hotels and boarding-houses, living out of suitcases, some-how cramming the children in their school holidays into her own cramped staff quarters, until the divorce settlement eventually enabled her to open an establishment of her own in rented premises in South Kensington. It offered a second home to Anglo-Indian children shipped half-way round the world, as the young Brownells had been, to make their own way among strangers in a country they had never seen with a climate unimaginably different from the only one they knew.

The enterprise was a success in human, if not in commer-cial terms. Furniture came out of store. Linen, glass and silverware were unpacked. Standards were not lowered. One of the many lessons Sonia learned from her mother was the importance of putting on a front, the way in which minor details of presentation – pretty flowers, polished surfaces, gleaming china, good food (accompanied in the daughter's case by fine wine, and plenty of it) – could comfort and fortify a perturbed or fearful spirit. Sacrifice and loss were woven into the fabric of empire at no matter what cost to individuals. Parents had to endure the pain of separation. Children must learn to do the same. Schools were there to reinforce the process. But places like Mrs Dixon's boarding-house in Tregunter Road helped to min-imize the damage. Lonely children were offered kindness, understanding and, perhaps even more important, a defens-ive armour that gave protection to the timid, shrinking heart within.

As her mother's trusty second-in-command, Bay threw

herself into the common task of rebuilding their fractured family. Sonia, who had never known the secure affection that had surrounded her sister as a baby, took the opposite path. Her family and its values – religious, social, imperial – came to stand for everything that had blocked and damaged her growth. Her closest ally at home was still Michael, who confirmed her great expectations by winning an open scholarship to Ampleforth College in 1935. For years before that her sisters had had to sink or swim. Their difficulties at school seemed petty beside their mother's problems. The boarding system had been designed expressly as a binding element for colonial families like theirs, doubly so for the offspring of violent and unstable homes, facing an uncertain future with no base to call their own. School fees had to be scraped together at all costs. Uncles stumped up. Trust funds were raided. Settlements chipped in.

But there was a heavy price to be paid, at a fashionable, top-of-the-range school like the Sacred Heart, by the Anglo-Indian daughter of divorced parents with no money to speak of and no fixed address. Sonia wrote scathingly in later life about the double standard underlying a religious schooling that inculcated doctrines of purity, sacrifice and self-abnegation in its pupils while vigorously endorsing in practice the worldly alternatives of power and privilege, class and financial status. School was a battlefield for Sonia, and she emerged from it with a raging scorn that found its outlet ten years later in *Horizon*:

> *What can be termed the 'Jesuitical' education is perhaps the most perfect weapon devised for entrapping the child, for it respects the intellect and recognizes that emotion is many-edged and*

deliberately sets out to use these two manifestations for its own ends; no area of the human personality is safe from the priests' probing cauterization . . .

The impact on a vulnerable and sensitive small girl is chillingly re-created in Antonia White's *Frost in May*, one of the most celebrated school stories of all time, with a convent setting that is a barely disguised version of Roehampton's Sacred Heart. The author was an old girl (known to the school under her real name of Eithne Botting), who had left in disgrace four years before Sonia was born. The two subsequently made friends on the strength of their response to the powerful early conditioning both had at first accepted with alacrity, then taught themselves slowly and painfully to resist. The nuns, adepts in obedience and submission, were skilled at detecting defiance and crushing childish provocation. 'I'm so bored I wish I'd been birth-controlled so as not to exist,' Sonia once said in the hearing of a nun at a school hockey match. The sentiment came close to blasphemy. Worse still was the brazen invocation of a modern invention of the devil anathematized then and later by successive popes. The heroine of *Frost in May* was expelled for less.

However outraged she felt in retrospect, however fiercely she repudiated the nuns and their faith, Sonia knew well enough that she had been shaped for ever by her nine years at the Sacred Heart. 'Children who were ever truly pious in a Catholic childhood are apt to retain a nostalgia for the absolute,' she wrote drily, discussing Simone de Beauvoir's education in terms that applied closely to her own. Sonia's convent upbringing was ultimately responsible for her uncompromising honesty, and her no less unconditional loyalty (accompanied on occasion, as Stephen Spender pointed out, by its reverse, a quite spectacular disloyalty to friends who let her down by failing to live up to the high view she took of them). As she grew older, she developed her own inimitable version of the Works of Mercy. No one ever spent more time and energy or lavished more imagination on devising subtle, sweet and humorous ways to tend the sick and comfort the afflicted.

Non-Catholics were often puzzled to explain a mission that seemed self-evident to Sonia. It gave point and purpose to an existence that would have been, by her own account, blank indeed without that stern commitment to hard, disinterested and unremitting effort. Work was her substitute for faith. It was her tragedy that her early training also instilled, at an even deeper level, the implacable sense of inadequacy and guilt that drove her conscience. 'I am sure,' wrote her friend and fellow Catholic David Plante, 'that this conscience – imposed, after all, not on her by herself but by her Catholic teachers – destroyed her finally.'

Not that there was anything out of the way by the standards of the place and period about the general curriculum of the Sacred Heart. Like most girls' boarding-schools between the wars, it provided functional rather than academic training for prospective imperial wives and mothers. The regime was orderly, disciplined and patriotic (or snobbish, illiberal and conformist, depending on your point of view). Victorian assumptions about the inadvisability of education for girls were part of the structure. It would be another quarter of a century and more before girls at this sort of institution were expected to sit public examinations like their brothers. Universities were for freaks and blue-stockings. 'Intellectual children are cuckoos in the nest of the bourgeoisie,' wrote Sonia, who had been one.

In fact she was singularly lucky in the two enthusiastic young nuns who taught English at the Sacred Heart in her last two years. Mary Allpress had taken a first-class degree at Oxford, Bertha Maude was the first woman ever to win the coveted vice-chancellor's essay prize at the same university. Sonia read voraciously under their tutelage as she would do to the day she died. All the concentrated sensitivity, effort and feeling she might have given in other circumstances to family relations poured into a consuming and sustaining love of literature. Books remained ever afterwards her prime source of consolation, a present help in time of trouble and a fixed refuge from despair.

Sonia left school in 1935, winning the school-leaver's prize for an essay called 'Man is a Builder', which nodded primly at religious underpinning but located the arts firmly at the core of all constructive effort. Poets and painters held the key for Sonia long before she ever met one and, when it came to choosing between the two, she came down on the literary side. Artistic expression was paramount: 'music, painting and poetry provide the highest outlets for this need,' she wrote. 'Poetry . . . is the music and painting of the mind.' Nothing in this mild and decorous essay gave any inkling of the tempestuous Sonia who would represent her education a decade later as a riot of sound, scent and colour:

> *In the Catholic school all the senses are attacked, everything shines, candles and lamps, scarlet wounds twinkle out of the pictures of martyrs, incense creeps through the cracks and half-*

*open doors, the organ booms accompaniment, and ritual, with
its atavistic tom-tom calls, begins and rounds off every day.*

The Sacred Heart's two most notorious old girls caused
a sensation towards the end of Sonia's time at school. *Frost
in May* came out in 1933. Two years later the friend who
had made her stage début alongside the infant Sonia in
Calcutta hit the headlines in the West End. The image of
an unknown Vivien Leigh – starring in *Mask of Virtue*, about
to become a real-life heroine of true romance by marrying
Laurence Olivier – produced the same sort of instant impact
as Princess Diana's first legendary snapshot on the front
pages. Leigh's fragile heart-shaped face, long lashes and

*Sonia's old friend and schoolfellow, Vivien Leigh, who became
another great enchantress*

wistful dark eyes made her a national icon overnight, and the British newspapers reached frenzy when their latest discovery was ratified by Alexander Korda with a film contract for a staggering £50,000.

Neither development can have been lost on Sonia, who left school with her modest essay prize that summer. The intellectual escape route that might have provided an alternative to marriage and motherhood was barred to her. There could be no question of university, but her mother did the next best thing by packing her off for a year to French-speaking Neuchâtel in Switzerland. The plan was for her to board with a sister of the Protestant pastor, whose daughter Madeleine was the same age as she was, and take courses at the local commercial college in French literature and language. The nine months she spent in Neuchâtel stamped her permanently for good and ill.

French became from now on for Sonia the joyful, liberating language of freedom, opportunity and pleasure. In the spring, as the days lengthened and the Alpine meadows filled with flowers, she went sailing with Madeleine and two Swiss boys. The four teenagers (all seventeen except for one of the boys, who was a year older) landed on the far side of the lake for a picnic lunch one fine day in May, and were sailing back when the wind rose and the sky darkened. A sudden vicious squall slithered down the mountainside and capsized the boat. The boys managed to right it but high waves prevented their climbing back on board. They clung to the boat, supporting Madeleine between them, while Sonia – the only one of the party who could swim – struck out for the shore to fetch help.

She heard a shriek and turned back to see her companions

Sonia round about the time she left school

going under one by one. When she reached the boat again, the last boy grasped her and tried to drag her down with him. Unable to save him, pushing him away, fighting in his clutches for her life, she tore free as he went down for the last time. She struggled to keep her head above the icy water for another twenty minutes before a pleasure steamer picked her up, numb, chill and exhausted. The steamer brought her back to land, together with Madeleine's body, but the bodies of the two boys were missing. Sonia had to tell the family of her dead friend what had happened.

Mrs Dixon travelled out from England to bring her distraught daughter home. Sonia never forgot the terrible embrace of a convulsive male body stronger than her own, and its even more terrible consequences. Her brother

Michael (who grew up to become a distinguished psychiatrist) said it remained the single most traumatic memory of her life. Thirty-six years later, reviewing a book of short stories by Alberto Moravia, Sonia wrote of the idle, aimless lives of his Roman women who can make no use of their intelligence save to describe their stultifying situation, which only makes it more intolerable:

> *But how well they describe it! Often with the force of the trapped who have no alternative but to become traps themselves, like drowning people who struggle against their rescuers: and, as drowning people are said to do, they see everything leading to their predicament with absolute clarity. But what help is that to them?*

Sonia recovered physically, but emotionally nothing would ever be the same again. She could no longer make even a pretence at carrying out the duties expected of a marriageable girl filling in time until rescued by an eligible suitor. After a decade of turbulence the Dixon family had at last achieved a semblance of normality at 31 Tregunter Road. But the daily domestic routines that represented a triumph for her mother seemed a mockery to Sonia. She had lost not only her faith but all patience with the social virtues – stability, continuity, solidarity – that supported what now struck her as a hypocritical sham. She was sarcastic, sceptical, unyielding. There were scenes, confrontations and slammed doors. She became a misery to herself and to her mother. 'Either the child gives in,' Sonia wrote later of this stage of adolescence, 'and adopts the dual vision of his parents, or he sticks doggedly to the beliefs he was taught, and after the usual dismal period of tears and recrimination, he leaves his family to find comfort and confirmation elsewhere.'

The family compromised by stumping up once again, for a secretarial course. Sonia, competent in all she did like her mother before her, became a fast and accurate typist. She was quickly bored with her first job but her employer, who knew when he was on to a good thing, refused to release her from her contract until she outmanœuvred him by adding the office telephone number to the figures at the bottom of an invoice. She had found a room of her own by this time on the borders of Fitzrovia, between Bloomsbury and Marylebone, a raffish hinterland of mean shops, bars and cafés bounded to the north by the Euston Road and to the south by Soho.

This was the territory of painters and poets, drifters and deadbeats from the shabbier end of the artistic and intellectual spectrum who hung out in pubs like the Wheatsheaf, the Fitzrovia and the George. It might have been a different planet from the Dixons' safe haven in South Kensington. Sonia's combination of innocence, eagerness and dewy freshness guaranteed male escorts. But now for the first time she met girls of her own age who had slipped the constraints of conventional society, like Dylan Thomas's girlfriend, Caitlin Macnamara, and Augustus John's daughter, Vivien. They talked as freely as men, wore high heels and lipstick, arranged their days to suit themselves, and survived haphazardly on hand-outs or their intermittent earnings as chorus girls, film extras, artists' models and painters in their own right.

In the summer of 1938, Sonia celebrated her flight from

the past with an escapade that would have appalled her family if they had been informed. She set out with two of her new men friends for Eastern Europe. Their destination was bandit country, best known to the British public between the wars for its swashbuckling Ruritanian royalty, or its Gothic castles full of mad counts and murderous vampires. It would have been unwise at the best of times for an inexperienced nineteen-year-old convent girl to tour the Balkans with two men she hardly knew. But in 1938 the region was on the brink of war (Czechoslovakia, under threat ever since Hitler had seized Austria that spring, reached crisis point amid international uproar in September, when war itself was temporarily postponed at the last minute by Neville Chamberlain in Munich).

Sonia's companions were a Russian, Serge Konovalov, and his friend, Eugene Vinaver, a Pole born and brought up in St Petersburg. Serge and Eugene spoke French with Sonia. Both men were twice her age. Both were more than half in love with her. Cosmopolitan, chivalrous and protective, they saw it as their role to shield her from rough and predatory advances. The two had started out together as brilliant young scholars sharing digs at Oxford university. Serge would eventually become Professor of Russian at Oxford; Eugene was already running the French department at the university of Manchester. They planned to spend the vacation with another couple exploring Yugoslavia, Bulgaria and Rumania in search of gypsy bands from the mountain towns and villages. Sonia said they also visited Poland where, according to her brother, she was chiefly struck by the Poles' unbudgeable conviction that they were about to conquer the world.

They travelled by car with Eugene (who had never driven before) at the steering-wheel. He would dine out afterwards on stories of their hair's-breadth escapes. Once a pack of wolves pursued them through a pine forest, another time they were imprisoned in a Rumanian gaol and had to sell the car-tyres to buy their way out. Twelve months later, when war was finally declared, Sonia would find herself threatened with arrest again by an East Anglian policeman, who suspected her of spying on the strength of the fancy foreign stamps in her passport.

If the party did in fact reach Poland, they would have been hospitably received by the Vinavers. Eugene had quantities of cousins, aunts, uncles and great-uncles in Warsaw. He was a charming, witty, charismatic character from a highly cultivated, liberal Jewish family unlike anything Sonia had come across before. His father was Maxim Vinaver, lawyer, statesman and radical reformer, the leader of East European Jewry in its fight for civil rights, and one of the founders of Russia's first democratic party in 1905. He had held a key post – alongside the father of the novelist, Vladimir Nabokov – in Kerensky's provisional cabinet after the revolution of 1917. When the Bolshevik army reached Sebastopol, the future author of *Lolita* escaped with the future Oxford scholar on the ship carrying their fathers into exile.

The young Vinaver (like the young Nabokov) turned his back on the political struggles that had ended in failure, loss and civil war. Max Vinaver had lived for years under threat of assassination or arrest by the Tsarist authorities before being forced by the Soviets to flee St Petersburg in disguise with Eugene. The son had had his fill of sudden flights, shots, police searches and interrogations. Politics had cost his family dear in private and in public. When the Vinavers eventually settled in Paris (which remained ever afterwards Eugene's favourite city), he abandoned the legal studies planned for him by his father to plunge headlong into the absorbing and exacting disciplines of medieval scholarship.

If anyone could sympathize with Sonia's situation, it was Eugene, whose family had always taken the education of girls for granted. One of his aunts had been among the first women doctors to qualify in Russia; his sisters and cousins were highly successful professional women. He too, like Sonia, had been uprooted early. He, too, had cut himself off from his family, when he crossed the Channel at twenty to start again at Oxford in a new language and another country. He knew how it felt to contend alone with hardship, poverty and isolation. Having made his own way with nobody to depend on but himself, he did what he could to help Sonia make hers. His base was Manchester, but he helped pay her weekly rent in London (according to her brother Michael, it came to four shillings) by offering her a typing job at £3 a week. The text he wanted her to type out was the Winchester manuscript of Thomas Malory's *Morte d'Arthur*.

This semi-legendary manuscript had been discovered by chance in dramatic circumstances four years earlier. Vinaver had beaten off stiff competition to be appointed editor of a text that would become, in his hands, the foundation stone of Arthurian scholarship to this day. He worked on the manuscript for twelve years, using a typescript transcribed in the first instance from photographs of the original text. There is no way of telling which of the precious folios

Eugene gave to Sonia, who already looked at nineteen as if she had stepped straight out of Malory's romance. She had luxuriant pale gold hair, the colouring of a pink and white tea-rose, and the kind of shapely, deep-breasted, full-hipped figure that would have looked well in close-fitting Pre-Raphaelite green velvet.

Eugene was not the only one to be enchanted by her. She also cast her spell over a band of young painters from a newly founded art school, which moved at the beginning of 1938 to premises above a disused car salesroom and repair shop at 314–16 Euston Road. The painters used to wave at Sonia through the window of her room, in a block behind the school, on their way to and from the studio. Lawrence Gowing, who would end up running the Slade School of Art, was a pupil. He never forgot seeing Sonia at her window, combing her long fair hair behind the dusty glass and looking up tentatively at the painters as they passed.

They longed to paint this shy and silent maiden whose identity no one knew, and whose mystery seemed even more romantic when they realized she was under the protection of a handsome Pole. William Coldstream – a future pillar of the British artworld, and one of the Euston Road School's three founders – climbed out of the studio skylight on to the roof with the painter Graham Bell in an attempt to arrest her attention. Their plan was to tap on her window and entice her upstairs to pose for them. It took several forays before they eventually succeeded and, when they did, Sonia's new admirers were intrigued to find that her Polish visitor was none other than the learned Professor Vinaver, keeper of the famous Malory manuscript that had made such a stir in the press a few years before. They were

Sonia in Regent's Park, *painted by one of the Euston Road School's founders, Claude Rogers, at the time when she was typing out the manuscript of Malory's* Morte d'Arthur

even more surprised to hear that the professor had entrusted the task of transposing his treasure to a recently qualified young typist on the Euston Road.

But Eugene was impressed by the accuracy of Sonia's transposition. He complimented her in business-like English, switching midway through his letter to charming, eager French to say that, although he felt half dead from overwork, he counted on the mere sight of her to restore him as if by magic. He could hardly wait to catch the train from Manchester to London on Friday night, when he would break all speed records by taxi over the short distance from Euston station to Sonia's street door, which he begged her to leave on the latch. Meanwhile his thoughts raced ahead of the few days that still separated them.

Eugene's visits made Sonia glow with happiness, according to Serge Konovalov, who instantly grasped the situation when they met in the local pub. Sonia was sufficiently impressed to jot down his reaction years later in notes for what seems to have been an abandoned memoir: 'Drinking beer in Charlotte Street pubs. Vivien John. Their lovers. Serge saying in Wheatsheaf, *"Mais que tu es devenue belle"* ["Well, haven't you grown pretty"]. My not understanding what he really meant.'

If Sonia's appeal for Eugene is easy to imagine, so is his for her. He was not only attentive, kind and entertaining. He was an intellectual with a formidably powerful and enquiring mind, already a leader in his field, who would go on to become the undisputed emperor of French medieval studies in his adopted country and in the United States. He represented a whole world of thought and learning Sonia had never before encountered outside books.

Nor for that matter had she ever known an older man on whom she could rely. 'My own father had died when I was six months old, my stepfather had gone mad, and there had never been anyone who "looked after me" in my life,' she wrote shortly before she died, explaining her blind faith in the accountant to whom she had confided her affairs. One of the recurring patterns in her life was the formation of strong and intimate friendships with men of great charm and natural authority, generally older than herself, whose intellectual distinction she revered, and who were in turn enthralled by her.

The affair with Vinaver, if it was one, proved short-lived. Sonia had neither the inclination nor the temperament for the role of scholar's wife (Vinaver would meet and marry his ideal helpmeet in 1939). But that brief encounter reached far and deep into her life. It confirmed her love of the French language and of France, especially of Paris, and it left her with a passionate admiration for the Jewish people that she never lost. Vinaver was the founding president of the international Arthurian Society, first conceived in 1930 at Truro in Cornwall, and finally constituted after the war at Quimper in Brittany. When Sonia visited these places with Michel Leiris in the 1970s, she was treading in the footsteps of a guide who had opened many doors for her; and perhaps she remembered what Vinaver's own first mentor, the Parisian scholar Joseph Bédier, had written when the younger man hesitated to leave Oxford for Manchester at the start of his career: 'Have no fear – the Knights of the Round Table will follow you.'

PART TWO

The Euston Road Venus

Sonia painted by William Coldstream
(photo taken for her by the artist)

The first of the painters to lure Sonia out from behind her window-pane was Adrian Stokes, who picked her up during a ballet in the gallery at Covent Garden. He took her to one of the famous parties at Bertorelli's restaurant on the Tottenham Court Road, where the Euston Road School of Art celebrated its successes at long tables laid end to end with wine, speeches and rowdy singing. Sonia told a friend long afterwards that she had been very close to Adrian for three weeks, but stopped seeing him when he turned nasty (the nastiness apparently consisted in his wanting to whisk her off to Venice, or alternatively – a joke that presumably turned sour – lock her in a cellar). When Adrian married a fellow painter in July 1938, Sonia went to the wedding, feeling unaccountably put out.

But her first regular beau was Victor Pasmore, one of the school's three founders, who painted and taught there every day. Pasmore lived in an attic above the White Tower restaurant at the top of Charlotte Street, with a commanding view down the long straight thoroughfare that cut through the heart of Fitzrovia to the Euston Road at the far end. From his window you could see painters going in and out of rented rooms up and down the street. This was the world of art and poetry Sonia had longed for all her life. Pasmore painted her, and so did his co-founders, Bill Coldstream and Claude Rogers (Sonia is one of two women on a bench in

Rogers' *Women and Children in the Broad Walk, Regent's Park*: the other was his wife Elsie).

The school, which prided itself on offering an alternative to the tyranny of European Modernism, was a rebel offshoot of Old Bloomsbury. The painters, Vanessa Bell and Duncan Grant, were staunch supporters in spite of lifelong allegiance to the pictorial values of the Post-Impressionists, first championed before the 1914–18 war by Roger Fry, who stood for everything the young Euston Roaders hoped to dislodge. Vanessa's sister, Virginia Woolf, signed cheques at fundraising parties for the new school thrown by Fry's companion, Helen Anrep. The two young Anreps, Baba and Igor, were regulars at the Café Conti on Charlotte Street, where teachers and pupils met for coffee most mornings before work. Soon Sonia was dropping in at these breakfasts too.

This was her first encounter with the denizens of Bloomsbury, old or new, and she was in some ways a cuckoo in their nest. Then and later they could always scent the whiff of an imperial and convent background that clung to her no matter what she did. Her love of absolutes made her too loud, too vehement, too sweeping in her protestations. People from more literary or artistic backgrounds – aesthetically more sophisticated, socially more uninhibited, intellectually more enquiring than her own – made her nervous. They in turn often thought her cocksure or pretentious.

Her looks didn't help. Sonia was no painter, but she wasn't a professional model either, and she never took her clothes off to pose for the life class in the nude. The nickname the painters gave her – the Euston Road Venus – was both flattering and ironic. She was half tickled, half unnerved to find herself being toasted as the Euston Venus in the pubs and bars around Charlotte Street by Basil Jonzen, who stood for everything the school deplored. Jonzen was a bestselling, high-profile painter – 'the great bohemian of our generation,' wrote Claude Rogers tartly – familiar throughout Fitzrovia for his big black hat, swirling cape and silver-topped cane. He specialized in flamboyant gestures that matched his theatrical costume, first worn by Parisian

Sonia on the Boulevard St Germain in Paris with
the poet Robert Waller

artists getting on for a century before. When Jonzen proposed marriage, Sonia turned him down (as she did most proposals in these years, regular or irregular).

In April 1939 she crossed the Channel again, this time with four painters: Graham Bell and his girlfriend Olivier Popham, Rodrigo Moynihan and his wife, Eleanor Bellingham-Smith. Sonia fell in love with Paris. A photograph shows her on the Boulevard St Germain near the

Deux Magots, the Café Flore and the Brasserie Lipp, around the corner from the rue des Saints Pères and the Hôtel Jacob: the beat that ten years later would become her second home.

The party was joined in Paris by another familiar figure from Fitzrovia, a poet called Robert Waller who took such a violent fancy to Sonia that he could not be shaken off, trailing them home via Rouen and the Channel ferry at Dieppe, where he was reluctantly persuaded by Olivier Popham to abandon his intention of rooming with Sonia above the Café des Tribuneaux. Once back in London, Olivier's lover, Graham Bell, rented a couple of rooms in Howland Street at the corner with Fitzroy Street, which he shared with Bill Coldstream. The two were old friends and, while Graham painted Olivier at Howland Street that summer, Bill painted Sonia.

Commercially a far less successful artist than Basil Jonzen, Coldstream was beginning to make a far more serious mark. Sonia liked his faintly dilapidated charm. 'Bill. His seedy dash, scruffy but somehow smart,' she wrote appreciatively in her notebook long afterwards. 'Bad teeth, good hands, a ring I think . . .' He was lean, wiry, loose-limbed and fine-boned, with floppy hair and the slight stoop ('not really an apologetic one,' Sonia noted shrewdly) often adopted by gentle, self-deprecating Englishmen of his generation to mask steely ambition.

He was ten years older than Sonia, with a wife and two small daughters whom he had just left. The Coldstreams had long been a semi-detached couple (Bill's wife Nancy was conducting an affair with the poet, Louis MacNeice: 'useful for taking her off your hands,' said Bill's old friend,

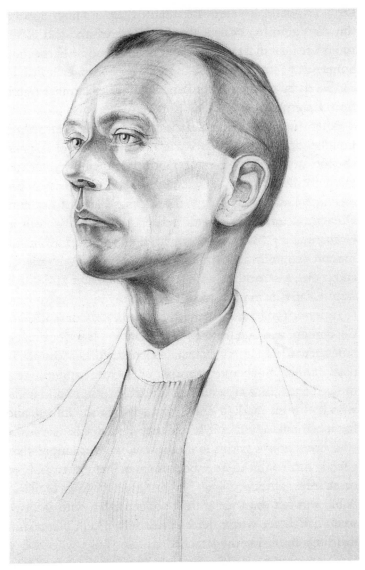

William Coldstream by Merlyn Evans

the poet W. H. Auden). Bill said he got to know Sonia a few days after her twenty-first birthday, which stuck in his mind because of the gold watch given her by her mother. Sonia was twenty-one on 25 August 1939. The portrait sittings can barely have begun when war with Germany was declared on 3 September.

After the false alarms and excursions of the year before, London anticipated immediate heavy bombing. Air-raid shelters stood ready, gas masks awaited distribution, evacuation got under way. Baba Anrep took Sonia down to her mother's house, Rodwell, in the Suffolk village of Bayham, already occupied by Claude and Elsie Rogers as well as Graham and Olivier. The long-awaited outbreak of hostilities proved an anticlimax. 'Beginning of war. "We must all carry on as if nothing unusual was happening,"' Sonia wrote flatly in her notebook. Nothing did, except that Claude and Graham excavated a slit trench at the bottom of the garden, and dug up the flowerbeds to plant vegetables.

It seemed like a Ruritanian comedy when a couple of plain-clothes policemen turned up before anyone was dressed one Sunday morning to interrogate Sonia and Baba, who had been marked down as suspect in the village pub for loose talk about not being prepared to kill Germans. The household's patriotic credentials were unimpressive. Claude turned out to have been born in Buenos Aires, Elsie came from Jamaica, Olivier had just got back from Holland, Baba and her mother were both stateless with Nansen passports, while Sonia herself had only recently returned from reconnoitring the Balkans.

The two girls left in a police car. They were released later the same morning (after the intervention of a neighbour,

Count Benckendorff, whose German name somehow re-assured the detectives), but not before Claude and Graham had infuriated Baba by burning her Trotskyite newspapers in an attempt to get rid of incriminating evidence. The episode was absurd but salutary. It marked the end of the life they knew. 'Rodwell. The arrest. Benckendorffs –' ran Sonia's cryptic note: 'Baba's severity with police – the shaving off of beards.'

The Euston Road School promptly closed, and the painters dispersed. Bill, waiting to be called up by the army, found a temporary post teaching art at Canford School in Dorset ('All the damned boys are smoking in their parents' cars outside the window –' he wrote fretfully to Sonia, 'Oh Lord!'). Sonia herself moved into the Moynihans' house at Monksbury in Hertfordshire, where she gave lessons to their small son, sat for Rodrigo and took him for walks, discussing art, life, death and his love for another painter's wife. When Bill came down for the weekend, Sonia would cycle into Bishop's Stortford to meet his train. He wooed her with parcels of pink sweets and bunches of red roses ('Lovely flowers he would send'). He wrote her courtly letters – 'Goodbye Sonia darling, and remember that as you excel in beauty I shall be rewarded for love' – carefully concealing his identity under a false hand on the envelopes. The Moynihans made Sonia smile with their efforts to marry her off that autumn.

At the beginning of December she came up to town to meet Bill secretly in London. 'Sonia dearest – you did look so thrilling curled up at 5 o'clock –' he wrote afterwards, having risen before dawn to catch his train back to Dorset, 'positively drenched in glamour and most awe-inspiring . . .

the streets were pitch black – not a taxi anywhere . . . ' Their affair was peripatetic as well as clandestine, conducted at snatched meetings in spare rooms or temporary lodgings among people constantly moving on, passing through, marking time or tiding themselves over while waiting to be mobilized. It was getting harder to live from hand to mouth. Sonia, who was even worse off than usual, landed a part-time post teaching the child of a wealthy foreign family in Hampstead. It meant she could afford a room in Goodge Street, where she started spending half the week.

Bill returned to his half-finished portrait, completing it around the corner in Vanessa Bell's old studio at 8 Fitzroy Square in the Christmas holidays. He painted Sonia leaning on one hand, in warm, glowing flesh tints with full red lips and a mass of pale, corn-coloured hair loosely pinned on top of her head. She looks like one of Renoir's plump, tousled, pink-flushed girls, except that her stare is both more provocative and more guarded. Already there was something daunting as well as dauntless about Sonia. Bill was captivated by it. 'Darling, do be gay & saucy & rather awe-inspiring too,' he wrote in a formula that became the refrain of their affair.

She loved his style, his malicious wit, the long walks they took together, and the heightened visual sense she got from being with him. She remembered a day in the country in winter snow, and what seems to have been a spring visit to Dorset ('that evening with white flowers & black beeches, near Weymouth – on downs'). But above all she loved him for his skill, his knowledge, his authoritative eye. He drew her, and they spent a great deal of time looking at and talking about painting. Sonia was absorbed, attentive, a

Bill Coldstream's drawing of Sonia Asleep

quick learner, and nothing if not thorough. She explored the National Gallery, made notes for Bill on Raphael, read Delacroix's *Journals*.

The young Euston Roaders had turned their backs on what they thought of as Modernism's excesses, rejecting Matisse, Picasso and the Post-Impressionists in favour of a generation of pioneers old enough to be their grandfathers. Cézanne and Degas were their gods. A passage from Sonia's notebook might almost be Bill Coldstream speaking: 'Philosophy of the Euston Road School. Anti-continental – Picasso the enemy. Impressionists the friends and teachers ... Henry Moore as enemy. Exhibition at Oxford. Mrs Anrep's hat bobbing in indignation at praise of Henry Moore.'

Soon Sonia had absorbed all Bill had to tell her about the contemporary British school, which was to feature in one of the early numbers of a new magazine already making waves in London. *Horizon*, launched in January 1940, would exert an influence far beyond anything its founders could realistically have envisaged at the start. Its commitment to artistic excellence, its rare combination of extreme sophistication and absolute faith in the rightness of its values, above all its confidence in the literature of the present, the past and by implication the future, were tonic at a time when civilization itself appeared to be on the verge of extinction. *Horizon*'s impact as a beacon in wartime, and its brief but crucial role in 1945 as a focal point for European cultural reconstruction, would be difficult to exaggerate.

In the autumn of 1939, the magazine was still in the planning stages, but its fame had already reached Bishop's Stortford. Sonia had heard gossip about goings-on at the London office of *Horizon* by November. 'I was very jealous until I realized they were all about 20 [this was a bit rich coming from someone who had just turned twenty-one] and thought Erik O'Day was a good painter,' she wrote saucily, urging Bill to keep an eye on one of *Horizon*'s editors, the poet Stephen Spender, who was planning a special issue on the latest developments in painting. 'I don't trust Spender's or Cyril Connolly's views on Art.'

Horizon's two literary editors were admittedly no great connoisseurs of modern painting, but Spender (himself briefly a pupil at the Euston Road School) was sufficiently intrigued by Sonia's impudence to commission a blueprint from her for the proposed Young Painters Number. More than sixty years on, it is still a perceptive and even-handed survey, laid out with clarity and skill, by no means wholly favourable ('the main body of English painting now is a negative sort of realism with a dash of Impressionism thrown in'), and certainly not biased in Coldstream's favour.

It showed imagination (one of Winston Churchill's essays was to be reprinted to give a brisk layman's survey of the historical position) harnessed to a journalist's ability to digest a broad range of new material, pick out the salient factors, and present them in a format at once entertaining and authoritative. Potential contributors ranged from Coldstream and Pasmore to Henry Moore, John Piper and Graham Sutherland. Professional art critics were to be assessed in a report – 'this could be boisterous or funny or sarcastic or wild' – by an astute outsider like John Betjeman, or Connolly himself. The number would end with a young painters' index (names, ages, average prices) and a page of small ads, each offering an individual work for sale in no more than twenty words (given *Horizon*'s unique impact, this scheme could have revolutionized access to the home art market in Britain).

The contents of the art issue would in short have been invaluable today, if the editors hadn't taken Sonia out to lunch at the Café Royal in April 1940 and turned her proposal down. The trouble was that there were three of them. The third was the paper's financial backer, Peter Watson, who had lived for years in Paris collecting de Chirico, Klee, Gris, Miró and Picasso. Watson, who had hoped to found an avant-garde Paris-based replacement for Christian Zervos's legendary *Minotaure*, had only reluctantly agreed to finance an English literary review instead. Neither Spender nor Connolly, as Sonia rightly said, knew or cared much about the main stream of contemporary painting, but Watson wasn't inclined to waste space exploring the work of a British school that struck him as insular and half-baked.

The editors would make *Horizon* famous for its bold, fresh, unconventional approach, but even they must have felt it would be going too far to engage as guest editor a twenty-one-year-old girl of no professional standing whatsoever. Spender had only asked her in the first place because Kenneth Clark (who had agreed to do it) had left them in the lurch by getting himself seconded to the new Ministry of Information. The art number was quietly dropped. Both Connolly and Watson would change their minds later, coming to endorse Spender's intuition and, after his departure, to rely heavily at *Horizon* on the quality of Sonia's editorial flair and judgement.

The shock to her at the time was great. The painter Francis Bacon, afterwards one of Sonia's closest friends, maintained that any belief she might have had in herself as a writer was irreparably damaged by this rejection. On the one hand, it reinforced her overriding faith in the importance of art and artists, more especially of writing and writers. 'It is as if for Sonia man could do nothing greater than write books,' wrote David Plante on first meeting her as a young novelist almost three decades later. But, on the other hand, the experience of being passed over by the literary world's sharpest umpires confirmed at some basic level of her being a sense of her own worthlessness.

The 1930s job market, regulated to ensure that women earned less than men and occupied subordinate positions, relied at all levels on cheap or unpaid female labour. *Horizon* could not have survived without it. Sonia continued helping out at the magazine's makeshift offices in Spender's flat in Bloomsbury, while she tried to find some sort of war work throughout the spring and summer of 1940. She typed, ran errands and did odd jobs for Spender, who occasionally produced her trainfare in return out of the petty cash. 'I can't bear talking about jobs,' she explained to Bill, who had protested about an attitude to money that would have increasingly serious, eventually disastrous repercussions for Sonia in later life: 'It's a terrible thing but when money is mentioned for work I just can't cope with it. Specially not with Stephen, whom I find it difficult to talk to anyhow.'

Spender struck her as funny and friendly but frighteningly high-powered. 'I can never quite feel at ease or natural with him,' she wrote to Bill that summer, 'because I feel a most innocuous remark might lead him to undress one's character entirely!' Her instincts were correct. Spender was fascinated by a profound ambivalence in Sonia, who seemed to him to be sending out the same mixed signals as she does in Coldstream's portrait. He never forgot his first impression of her: 'round Renoir face, limpid eyes, cupid mouth, fair hair, a bit pale perhaps. She had a look of someone always struggling to go beyond herself, to escape from her social background, the convent where she was educated, into some pagan paradise of artists and "geniuses" which would save her.'

Stephen Spender painted by William Coldstream

In a sense it did. 'She lives in terms of others' creativity,' Bacon said long afterwards: 'she has no illusions about being creative herself.' But the gulf between reality and dream was hard to accept at first. In 1939, Bill Coldstream was the closest Sonia had yet come to genius, apart from Spender himself ('a rattle-headed, bolt-eyed young man, raw-boned, loose-jointed,' Virginia Woolf noted in her diary the day they met, 'who thinks himself the greatest poet of all time'). The snag was that what all these artists – geniuses or not – needed was a wife, which nearly always turned out in practice to mean someone to see to the laundry, clean up the room, do the shopping and keep track of bills.

Most of the painters Sonia knew had made early marriages to fellow painters that were by this time splitting up. Neither home nor school provided training in elementary domestic skills for young husbands struggling to make a first mark on the artworld. Childbearing almost invariably meant it was the wives' careers that foundered. Unattached men lived in regal squalor, dining out in cheap eateries and relying on landladies to stem the rising tide of dust and debris. Sonia's chief memory of the housekeeping at Howland Street was of Bill and Graham peeing into empty milk bottles (Olivier, who also came across this row of bottles, thought they contained linseed oil).

Sonia's mission may have been to help more creative practitioners than herself, but when one of them suggested the obvious way – 'make a good wife for an artist' – her reaction was outrage. She herself couldn't make a cup of coffee in those days, let alone cook a meal. Over the next twelve months or so she tidied Bill's studio for him, washed his dirty linen ('how are you off for socks?'), posted him jam and biscuits. Male helplessness always had its funny side for Sonia. But she found it hard to stomach the automatic assumptions that went with it about the inferiority of girls: 'they were not to be considered quite on a par with men when it came to making up a list for an exhibition,' explained Claude Rogers (whose own wife Elsie cut up very rough indeed when he embarked, round about this time, on the first of many extramarital affairs): 'Coldstream was very peculiar at times on this subject.'

First-hand observation did not encourage rushing into marriage. Bill's divorce was in the pipeline, Spender got his in 1940, the Stokes' and the Moynihans' would come through a few years later. The Rogerses (who remained together for four decades) were locked in battle. 'She suffers very acutely from the disease common to all artists' wives,' wrote Sonia, totting up the various ways in which marriage soured Elsie's temper and cramped her vision as an artist: 'She has suffered so much from identifying herself with Claude and his career and from the life of Charlotte Street that her judgement becomes obscured . . . & she is mean & nasty & always on the defensive.' Becoming a second wife to Bill, fondly as he doted on his dear sweet darling little Sonia, looked like a project that could usefully be shelved.

Sonia solved her immediate financial problems by getting a job at the end of July 1940 with a Mobile First Aid Unit attached to University College Hospital. She pored over First Aid manuals, and dressed up in unbecoming white overalls: 'I've bought my uniform and look very bogus in it.' But the sense of sham and play-acting, widespread in Britain in the first year of war, would not last much longer. Bill was finally called up to join his artillery regiment in Dover, and Sonia saw him off from Waterloo on 13 August. Hitler, who had occupied Poland, allied himself with Italy and Russia, defeated Belgium, Holland and France, was now poised to cross the Channel.

'The Invasion . . . will probably take place within the next fortnight,' Sonia warned Bill cheerfully: 'If it does I do

Sonia: polyfotos taken in the summer of 1940 to send to Bill when he left to join the army

hope they don't choose Dover as their starting off point.' The bombs falling intermittently on London would soon become continuous. From early September Sonia's letters became bulletins of explosions, booming anti-aircraft guns and dogfights over Charlotte Street. More than 10,000 tons of bombs fell on the City of London in a single night. 'Well we're absolutely in the midst of it now,' wrote Sonia: 'The East End has been on fire for the last two nights and after dark all the sky is lit up and the buildings as far away as here are pink with the reflection . . .' Bombs dropped on Baker Street and Camden Town. People retreated underground by night ('They've got the most lovely Air Raid shelters under Faber with rows and rows of books to read'), emerging next morning on to streets full of smashed glass and broken buildings.

Sonia worked day and night in shifts, accompanying the rescue crews who dug out bodies from the rubble. The survivors were crushed, maimed, sometimes unconscious, often gassed. Once she watched two rescue men slowly and patiently excavating their own families from a collapsed tenement at King's Cross. Another time they found a man under the ruins of a block in Windmill Street, stark naked but still inexplicably alive. Mostly the bodies they brought out were dead. Sonia grew to hate the sleeping quarters provided in the hospital basement. 'I've seen too many people dug out of basements lately,' she wrote, after a particularly hard night's bombing on Fitzrovia: 'Goodnight darling, I wish we were in a lovely hotel in Dieppe with red carpets & wallpaper & a large fourposter bed.'

Sonia celebrated her birthday on August 25 with a surprise visit from her mother (who was rising rapidly up the ranks in the ATS), and an exhilarating night on the hospital roof watching the bombs fall, 'the sky all pink & the balloons gleaming in it'. Bill said that Sonia was absolutely fearless in an air raid (he himself claimed to have spent an hour in the Tube, shuttling between Goodge Street and Warren Street stations until sirens sounding the all-clear signalled it was safe to come out). She moved into one of the rooms above the White Tower in Percy Street and, when he sent flowers, wrote to report a bomb at the corner of the road: 'my room is now the perfect wartime room with no windows & red roses.'

By the middle of September virtually everyone she knew had left the district except for Elsie Rogers in Russell Square, which had twice been roped off because of unexploded bombs. 'Elsie is now evacuated,' Sonia wrote: 'That means that I'm the only person who hasn't been evacuated yet though there was an incendiary bomb on Percy St this morning.' West End theatres had closed, most roads were blocked or cordoned off, movement in the blackout was difficult or impossible. 'All life has been killed by the Air Raids,' Sonia wrote: 'You can't imagine what London is like now. It is just steadily being destroyed, large lumps of houses fall down . . .'

People hung about on the pavement in Charlotte Street that autumn looking up at the bombers overhead. One morning, Sonia got up to find Fitzroy Street full of gaping holes, Mecklenburgh Square smashed and Brunswick Square on fire. Another morning, the north end of Tottenham Court Road had been destroyed with flames pouring out of Maples's furniture store. On 17 November, she looked out of her window after a fearful night to find the White Tower itself surrounded by craters and time bombs. Cyril Connolly, who had taken her out to lunch at the Café Royal the week before to sound her out about a job, had just offered her 30 shillings a week to work part-time as secretary for *Horizon*. 'Of course I'd like it very much,' Sonia wrote cautiously to Bill, 'but they may be frightened out of London after last night!'

In fact nothing so straightforward as wholesale destruction ever apparently fazed Connolly. One of his great gifts as an editor was his ability to carry on as if the war weren't happening. He lived the years 1940–45 at the time – and summed them up in retrospect – as one of those points in history 'when literature seemed to follow life like a barge on a quiet canal towed by a madman on a motor-cycle'. Connolly saw it as his role to remain unblinking at the barge's helm. It took nerve in the London blitz to insist that creative writing mattered as much as bedlam in Europe, but Connolly made few concessions. 'His movements like his voice were indolent, one had the impression that he should have been eating grapes, but at the same time his half-closed eyes missed nothing,' wrote Julian MacLaren-Ross (whose first short story was among *Horizon*'s best and earliest wartime discoveries): 'He was a formidable person.'

Cyril Connolly by Lucian Freud

If people were impressed by Connolly's laid-back approach to war, they marvelled even more at his appeal for girls like Sonia. *Horizon*'s office seemed at times to be almost entirely staffed by Cyril's wives and girlfriends. Their name was legion (Diana Witherby, Lys Lubbock, Joan Eyres-Monsell and Janetta Woolley were the staples). All of them were in some sense sports from the upper-middle-class typing pool, freelancing energetically between the constraints of school and marriage. All of them were more or less enthusiastically caught up in the complex machinery of Connolly's flirtatious and eventful love life. His male contemporaries saw him as a mirror image of the Ancient Greek king Pentheus, 'held together rather than torn apart by the Mænads,' in Anthony Powell's tart phrase.

Physically Connolly was tubby and unimpressive. Stephen Spender said he looked like a teapot without a spout. He was in his mid-thirties on the outbreak of war when *Horizon* started, and (like Winston Churchill with whom he had points in common) he had been preparing himself for years for precisely such an eventuality. 'His big face – flat blue eyes, tiny nose and double chin – looked ageless as a Buddha's,' wrote Christopher Isherwood, 'but he was more of a pope than a Buddha, for he spoke with conscious authority, implying that he knew you, as a writer, better than you knew yourself.'

Papal authority was something Sonia understood. Of all the bright, adoring and conspicuously pretty girls Cyril recruited to run *Horizon*, she was intellectually the toughest, and probably the most disinterested. She was nineteen or twenty when they first met (according to her notes, it was at dinner with Victor Pasmore, after which they dined out alone together so Cyril could tell her more about the book that made his name, *Enemies of Promise*). A decade later he sent her a playlet, *The Id Never Sleeps*, dramatizing that first meeting. Like many of Cyril's projects, it never got beyond the first page on which Sonia tap-dances saucily across the stage – 'doop a doop, doop a doop, doop a doop' – eyed greedily by a lascivious Cyril: 'When I think of you all those years ago . . . It chokes me . . . Heavens, how young you were!'

Cyril represented civilization in the lofty literary form Sonia had been looking for ever since she left school. He stirred her mind, and pierced her heart. He gave her the further education she had missed, and to her dying day she could recall her thrill of pride and gratitude. One of the funniest of Spender's innumerable, often apocryphal Sonia stories was the one about a weekend in the country with Connolly's friend Dick Wyndham, a leathery, lustful satyr who pursued her round his garden until she dashed into the pond. 'It isn't his trying to rape me that I mind,' she gasped when the writer Peter Quennell fished her out, 'but that he doesn't seem to realize what Cyril stands for.'

Gunner Coldstream had been promoted to second lieutenant shortly before Sonia officially joined *Horizon*, but their affair could not long survive this new enchantment. Bill came up to London as often as he could wangle leave. The two spent Christmas together in her room at the White Tower, and in March she took the train to Bristol, where he was busy camouflaging the West Country. But none of these encounters was much of a success. Sonia said afterwards that she had agreed to marry Bill on condition her name was kept out of his divorce proceedings and that, when he cited her, she broke off the engagement. She must have done it deftly, and as sweetly as she could, for Bill's last letter accepting her decision is resigned, regretful, and still full of admiration. 'You have always been generous & kind & gentle & gay,' he ended sadly: 'I love you Sonia. Bill.'

Things seem to have been more or less over between them by the time she reviewed an exhibition of Euston Road School painting at Oxford in the spring of 1941. Sonia's article in the May issue of *Horizon* was restrained and valedictory (unlike John Piper's, which compared the impact of this brave new British school to the shock of a damp sponge). At some point the same year she left *Horizon* to work for Connolly's only serious rival, John Lehmann, on *Penguin New Writing*. Perhaps money had something to do with it, since Sonia had by now been living for four years pretty much on air. Perhaps she was poached by Stephen Spender, who had divided his allegiance from the start between *Horizon* (which he, too, left in 1941), and the less prestigious but richer and more popular *New Writing*. In secretarial terms Sonia was already an editor's dream: glamorous, efficient, inexpensive, highly knowledgeable and sharp as nails, as Lehmann warmly acknowledged in his memoirs:

> *I had a great fondness for the pretty, blonde, vivacious Sonia with her darting, gaily cynical intelligence and insatiable appetite for everything that went on in the literary world: her revolt against a convent upbringing seemed to provide her in those days with an inexhaustible rocket fuel.*

Within a few months Sonia had been snapped up yet again by an alert talent-spotter at the Ministry of War Transport in Berkeley Square, where she would remain to the end of the war. The Ministry was strategically placed for Connolly's HQ at the Café Royal in Piccadilly. On the strength of her first regular job, Sonia took a flat at 18 Percy Street with two tiny rooms and a minute kitchen, a few doors away from the White Tower. Connolly and his current girlfriend moved in May 1942 to much grander premises nearby at 49 Bedford Square. Here they threw parties of unheard-of, sybaritic, prewar splendour at which half the contributions to *Horizon* were initially sparked off, and subsequently commissioned, from a glittering guestlist. 'Cyril's household, in these wartime surroundings, was a constant source of wonder,' wrote Peter Quennell: 'He kept the war at bay more effectively than any other man I knew.'

After the chaotic informality of a literary review, the Ministry must have been an eye-opener for someone who, like Sonia, was by nature and heredity a born manager. It was not for nothing that her mother (now a Brigadier in the ATS) had been known at the same age as Bossy Binning. Running other people's lives, solving their marital or domestic problems, straightening out the affairs of the nation were meat and drink to both of them. Both tapped fresh reserves of strength and energy in wartime. After long demanding days spent poring over shipping routes and bills of lading, Sonia emerged at night to dine with diplomats at the Ritz, or drink and dance with more raffish, arty friends at the Gargoyle Club on Dean Street in Soho.

War work, which brought out latent business acumen and administrative ability in so many women, gave Sonia a cool methodical professionalism. By 1945, when she returned as editorial secretary to *Horizon*, she was no longer the prewar ingénue, barely more than a schoolgirl, who had amused her male colleagues with what Spender called 'the extraordinary mixture of sophistication and naïveté in many things she said – her transparent longing to be in the intellectual aesthetic swim'. Sonia at twenty-seven was set to become a force to reckon with in the book world.

She played the role with poise and verve. She dressed

Sonia and Cyril at Horizon *(the two seated figures are George Orwell's friend, Tosco Fyvel, and Cyril's girlfriend, Lys Lubbock)*

demurely in plain dark skirts and sweaters with lace-collared white blouses, and wore her thick, shiny, ash-blonde hair swinging loose at shoulder level. But the smooth surface had an edge of provocation. Friends were taken aback by Sonia's vehement denunciations of the conventional bourgeois world from which she came. She wrote trench-antly about it in *Horizon*, and she told Diana Witherby that she still spat whenever she saw nuns passing on the street.

She could knock back gin cocktails and use strong lan-guage like a man. Her style of argument was rapid and incisive, reinforced by flashing smiles, emphatic nods and expressive hand movements. 'Who is that?' asked Anthony Powell, when he first saw her laying down the law at one of Cyril's parties. Powell, then a newly appointed, junior-ranking literary editor of *Punch*, was suitably impressed by the response he got from another ambitious young hopeful with his first foot on the literary ladder, the future editor of the *London Magazine*, Alan Ross: '*That is the great Sonia Brownell.*'

Powell would draw an affectionate portrait of Sonia as Ada Leintwardine in *Books Do Furnish a Room*, published in 1971. Ada's brisk efficiency, cutting judgement and shrewd grasp of literary pecking order all come from Sonia. So does her expert and supremely tactful handling of temperamental, older, invariably male colleagues. Sonia, who still revered Cyril, had by now learned how to manage him as well. 'Cyril fascinated her with his brilliance, funniness and non-stop desire for sympathy,' wrote Spender, describing Connolly's view of himself as the incarnation of cruelly frustrated creative genius. 'Understanding the many ways in which Cyril was misunderstood provided Sonia with a tremendous brief, which took up much time and energy.'

But, dearly as she loved Cyril, Sonia came to love his partner Peter Watson even more. Peter was constitutionally elusive – absence was part of his character, as Spender said – so much so that posterity has tended to downgrade him, or write him out of the editorial record altogether. But people who were present at the time all agree with Cyril's view that his relationship with Peter was the key to *Horizon's* brilliant, if erratic mechanism. Peter was exceedingly fastidious, and extraordinarily perceptive. Sonia responded unreservedly to his honesty, generosity and kindness, and perhaps even more deeply to the brooding melancholy that underlay his surface humour. Cyril said he always knew if his co-editor was in the office because, when Sonia opened the door, she gave him only 30 per cent of her smile, reserving the other 70 per cent for Peter.

The two were made, as Cyril said, to compromise. Where Cyril was short and podgy, Peter was slender, willowy and elegant. Where Cyril's wit flashed and crackled, Peter was quiet, slow-spoken, self-effacing. He was by all accounts irresistible to both sexes, with a string of boyfriends as striking as Cyril's girls. Peter's looks were sleek, subtle and in the nicest possible way reptilian, 'equally poised between the prince and the frog,' wrote the critic Alan Pryce-Jones. The painter Anne Dunn remembered him always in a mac, on the move, quick and unobtrusive as a lizard. Cecil Beaton (who was hopelessly in love with him for years) said he had the face of a charming cod-fish. Peter had a great deal of money (his father was the margarine magnate, Sir Norman Watson), modernist instincts in art, and a first-hand knowledge of contemporary French culture, all of which Cyril lacked. 'The essential feature of *Horizon* was dual control,' wrote Cyril. 'As Hardy, I emulated his despair, as Laurel, he financed my optimism.'

As editors they were both, to Cyril's satisfaction, invincibly amateur. Inexperienced, untrained, self-taught, they operated by fits and starts – 'long periods of intense energy interspersed with sloth' – improvising hit-or-miss techniques on an ad hoc basis. Sonia said their office management was at best higgledy-piggledy. Their opinions often clashed. It was amazing, as Cyril pointed out to *Horizon*'s readers in his first end-of-year report, that a magazine run by editors so incompetent and apparently so incompatible ever came out at all. In fact the partnership worked

Sonia's beloved friend and mentor, Peter Watson,
photographed by Cecil Beaton

smoothly because, in the first place, they complemented one another and, in the second, they shared the same clear, highly developed and exacting aesthetic standards. Cyril's taste was almost wholly literary, Peter's largely but by no means exclusively concerned with contemporary music and the visual arts.

Sonia's initial contribution to the workplace was stability and order. Sloth ceased to be a factor in the day-to-day running of the office. Queries were answered, manuscripts returned, proofs sent out on time. Contributions no longer got mislaid or thrown away. In the second half of *Horizon's* ten-year lifespan, Sonia was generally agreed to be, in practice if not in theory (as a colleague said of Powell's Ada

Leintwardine), 'the kingpin of the whole operation. Maybe I should say queen bee'.

Cyril and Peter, rightly regarding her as in some sense their own creation, were proud of Sonia's youth, energy and talent. The Euston Road Venus was definitely an asset at the parties *Horizon* gave after the war to celebrate, or welcome home, literary prodigies and potentates like Auden, Louis Aragon, Edmund Wilson and T. S. Eliot. As Sonia's grip grew firmer and more confident, the editors loosened theirs, monitoring her progress from a distance like a couple of favourite, fond uncles. Peter called her *Miel*, or Honey, and, as soon as the lifting of wartime restrictions enabled him to leave the country, kept her supplied with French perfume and silk stockings from America.

He put her in touch with a rising generation of post-Euston Road British painters roughly the same age as herself. During five years of enforced wartime confinement, Peter sought out, encouraged and subsidized young painters like Lucian Freud, John Craxton, Graham Sutherland and Francis Bacon, all of whom became Sonia's friends. The highly competitive Freud, who had first met Sonia as a schoolboy at the Moynihans' in the early stages of her affair with Coldstream, briefly succeeded him as her lover. The two remained afterwards on affectionate terms, often forming a trio with Francis Bacon on long drunken nights that ended at the Gargoyle. Francis shared Peter's love and knowledge of Paris, his concentrated response to literature, his surface elusiveness and underlying reliability for anyone in trouble. Of all her friends, Francis was the one who, after Peter's premature death in 1956, would come closest to filling his place for Sonia.

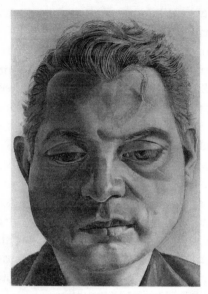

Francis Bacon by Lucian Freud

Peter believed, like Cyril, that England should look out-wards, to Europe and America, after the war, rather than retreat into introspection and nostalgia. In the first years of peace it was Peter who commissioned *Horizon* articles in Paris on artists barely known in Britain, like Balthus and Morandi. It was Peter who persuaded Picasso's dealer, Daniel Kahnweiler, to report on the contemporary art market, and Peter who coaxed Michel Leiris to write about his friend, Alberto Giacometti, whose elegant, elongated sculpture seemed unimaginably strange to unaccustomed eyes in those days. Sonia learned an immense amount from Peter and, being ten years younger, rapidly became the bolder of the two. Her unbridled modernity was a running joke between them. 'I may be more avant-garde than you soon!' Peter wrote, reporting an encounter with a trendy young Parisian philosopher for whom Jean-Paul Sartre's existentialism was already out of date.

Cyril meanwhile devoted inordinate amounts of time to completing Sonia's literary education. Anthony Powell's wife, Violet, once watched them walking down a street together in the early stages of this training, Cyril looking straight ahead with a small smile of satisfaction on his face, Sonia leaping up and gambolling about him 'like a Labrador puppy'. They talked non-stop about books, or rather Cyril talked and Sonia listened, absorbing his pronouncements as articles of faith. The implicit obedience she had learned as a child – and withdrawn at such cost from the Church's teaching – now went into observing Cyril's anathemas and imprimaturs. His admiration for Gustave Flaubert ensured that, to the end of her life, Sonia was apt to think most problems could be settled (as her brother Michael said) 'by a good quotation from Flaubert'. Cyril's dismissal of Victor Hugo meant she would be sixty before she permitted herself to so much as open one of Hugo's novels ('What a genius!' she wrote to me in 1978, four years after Cyril's death).

Editing *Horizon* gradually developed into a three-way working relationship. Cyril had tested out ideas on Peter from the start and Sonia now joined in, continuing the process by letter as the other two spent more and more time away from London. 'I think the Goyen story quite awful – old hat, D. H. Lawrence symbolism unimaginatively written,' Peter wrote severely to her about a contribution he hadn't chosen. He was crisper still in his postmortem on the magazine's special American issue in 1947: 'Phillips/Barrett/Greenberg/Soby – all competent. The poetry is good though I can't make out what Auden is doing at all . . . The Barzun is academic . . . Lamantia is very bad and *very* little magazine stuff, and Isherwood is dull. McLuhan excellent and both the stories quite good in that artless neo-reportage way . . .'

Sonia gave as good as she got in this sort of exchange, being often better placed than either of the other two to assess a manuscript. 'Nothing was ever a chore to her,' said John Craxton, who had watched her systematically trawling through every contribution that entered the *Horizon* office: 'When they argued, she fought for things. She was one of the great arbiters of that place. They turned to her. Sonia was the one who spotted people who were completely unknown.' Decisions were increasingly left to her. 'Do accept anything you think good,' Cyril wrote to Sonia in July 1948 from his summer station at Somerset Maugham's villa in the south of France. Her discoveries have been routinely claimed by Connolly's biographers ever since as feathers in his cap.

Perhaps the most impressive was Angus Wilson, first published by Sonia in *Horizon* long before the rest of the literary world knew him as anything but (in his own words) 'a rather tiresome, pretentious little man from the BM, at any rate on the surface'. Wilson was an Assistant Keeper in the Reading Room at the British Museum, when Sonia picked his short story, 'Mother's Sense of Fun', for publication in November 1947. Later, he decided she was too domineering, and got his own back by caricaturing her as the bossy, uningratiating Elvira Portway in his novel, *Anglo-Saxon Attitudes*. But when she eventually forgave him, he responded with a warmth and affection that lasted to the end of both their lives. 'You know, I hope, Sonia dear,' he wrote to her four months before she died, 'to what a degree and how constantly I remember that, but for you (and I think it was above all you) choosing one of my stories for *Horizon*, I should never have started a life of a writer.'

By 1947, Sonia had grown used to filling the pages for long periods on her own. From the first year of peace, Peter had been liable to disappear with little or no warning for weeks or months on end. Cyril had been even quicker off the mark, reaching Paris in January 1945, five months after the Liberation, to be 'fêted as though he were Voltaire returned', according to the British ambassadress Diana Cooper. A few years later he made an equally regal progress through New York ('Cyril's triumph here must be seen to be believed,' Peter wrote ruefully to Sonia: 'It's all too much for me'). Both of them spent summers in Italy or the south of France, leaving Sonia in London to bring out the magazine. 'She never grumbled or complained,' said the American writer, James Lord, another of the young unknowns who had his first short story picked by Sonia for publication in *Horizon*: 'She had the great gift of enthusiasm.' 'She was always there in the office,' said John Craxton. 'She was the rudder of that place.'

Her position, and the power it gave her, inevitably caused offence. She could be categorical and high-handed. Her interest in the visual arts, and in developments across the Channel, often seemed affected to more insular contemporaries. Her fondness for French words and phrases infuriated people who didn't speak the language. Natasha Spender told a nice story about Cyril dropping into cockney slang to say, when someone asked after Sonia (whose French was much better than his), that she was well but suffering from a bad attack of the parlay-voos. She had caught Cyril's trick of ranking authors and their books in order of precedence, and she upset rejected contributors by writing rather grandly using his editorial we. Dissatisfaction grew. Contributors to *Horizon*, as to all literary reviews in those days, were nearly always male, and men were not used to being told their performance was not good enough by a young woman.

She was blamed, mocked and derided. 'There was always some absurd Sonia story floating around,' wrote Stephen Spender. A body of myth grew up, sometimes harmless, often spiteful, damaging and untrue. 'Whenever things were hard, they simply sent Sonia out to sleep with a few advertisers or possible backers,' Spender himself was said to have told the publisher, John Calder. When Calder repeated his accusation in print after Sonia's death, Spender lodged a note in the Orwell Archive declaring it a fabrication, and insisting he had said nothing of the sort.

Much of the trouble was that Sonia was trespassing on traditionally masculine critical and intellectual preserves. 'It wasn't fair,' complained the hero of Louis Aragon's novel *Aurélien*, in a passage Sonia singled out in her *Horizon* review of November 1945: 'Women had a different kind of intelligence. They had no business meddling in affairs that didn't concern them.' Sonia's male contemporaries found it hard to credit that a woman with none of their advantages at school or university could have a brain as good as theirs. 'I think it was male vanity,' said Violet Powell, explaining why Sonia's intervention in the world of work caused such indignation at a time when girls were expected to keep their place (which, when not actually in the home, meant taking dictation in the office, answering the telephone and making tea). Sonia maintained a higher profile than her married women friends, who watched the male literary world retaliate in her lifetime and afterwards with sniping and sexual innuendo.

Her sex life provoked particular resentment. People never tired of speculating about it. Sonia favoured neither of the styles – discreetly butch, or austerely academic and asexual – conventionally adopted by more prudent professional women (still in those days mostly teachers). A tough shell had replaced her air of dewy innocence. She had always been a battler, and it was not in her nature to ingratiate herself with anyone seeking sexual favours. Cyril himself ranked Sonia second in his listings for sex appeal (first was his future wife, the beautiful, feral Barbara Skelton). When he failed to get her into bed, he put her down as lesbian.

Others, smarting from professional or sexual rebuffs, declared that she was frigid. The staff at *Horizon* got used to parrying advances from the ranks of Sonia's disappointed suitors. One was Julian Maclaren Ross, who grew so insistent that Cyril said he had to be barred as far as possible from the office 'on account of his grand passion for Sonia'. Another was the literary editor of the *New Statesman*, G. W. Stonier. A third was one of *Horizon*'s brightest stars, the *Tribune* columnist, George Orwell.

Sonia had first encountered Orwell at dinner with Cyril during her initial stint at *Horizon* in 1940 or 1941. By the time she met him again after the war, he was a widower struggling with incipient tuberculosis and the care of an adopted infant son. The author of *Animal Farm* was an

George Orwell with his son Richard

austerely romantic figure, tall, grey-faced and gaunt, 'like
St Christopher with the Christ child,' said Violet Powell,
who remembered him stalking bombed-out city streets
with the baby hoisted on his shoulder. Orwell complained to
his male friends of chronic loneliness after his wife's death
in 1945.

Sonia, nothing if not practical, offered to babysit the
child, Richard, on his nanny's days off while Orwell was

out on his journalistic rounds. She became one of several girls he hardly knew with whom he hoped in vain to share his life. Olivier Popham (who was another) lived in the flat below Orwell's in Canonbury Square. Dropping in on him one day in 1946, she was surprised to find Sonia already installed upstairs, entertaining her host with a tirade about Mallarmé and evidently making herself very much at home. The two got on well enough for Sonia to sleep with Orwell, more for his sake than hers, before explaining reluctantly (like all the other girls he asked at this stage) that she could not marry him.

She plunged back into her hectic London literary life, and Orwell retired that summer to the Hebridean island of Jura to recreate Sonia as Julia, 'the girl from the Fiction Department', in *Nineteen Eighty-Four*. The novel's hero, Winston, loves Julia for her boldness, her bossiness, and the uncompromising rejection of the Party that fuels everything she does. Julia's fearlessness electrifies him. Even the coarseness of her language strikes him as a symptom of revolt, 'natural and healthy like the sneeze of a horse that smells bad hay'. Winston's agonized intellectual reservations are overwhelmed by Julia's fierce, blind, animal abhorrence of a totalitarian system that seeks to abolish individuality and freedom.

Sonia herself confronted the nature and origins of this revulsion in *Horizon* in July 1946 in a lengthy review of Roger Peyrefitte's *Les Amitiés particulières*. Half her article was devoted to exploring with barely controlled fury the pain and humiliation of her own childhood defeats. Peyrefitte's novel centres on a particular friendship between two boys at a Catholic boarding-school, whose feelings for one another (like Winston's for Julia in *Nineteen Eighty-Four*) constitute subversion. The book inflamed memories already stirred by Orwell's curiosity about her schooling. Sonia came close to incoherence as she contemplated the authorities who had shaped her childhood with a:

> discipline . . . less interested in sex than in the danger which a private emotion threatens to their system. Two children who love each other create a world they cannot enter and their whole object is to control, utterly, every thought and feeling. Friendship must be healthy, i.e. boring, or it must be stamped out, but priests, like all totalitarians, forget that their methods can be adopted by the enemy. The intelligence they are training for one war can be used for another.

The article explores tortuous strategies of treachery, betrayal and what Orwell called doublethink, the 'double vision' Sonia diagnosed at the heart of a Catholic system administered by the religious equivalent of Orwell's thought police ('each separate child must be controlled, every secret corner of his heart disinterred, and to do this they tear away any belief in the support that one human being can give to another . . .'). There is probably no way of establishing whether or not Orwell read the July issue of *Horizon*, but it is hard to write off as coincidence the fact that, at the very moment when he started work on *Nineteen Eighty-Four*, his ex-mistress outlined in print precisely the scenario that would become the central section of his plot.

Like Sonia, the novel's heroine unequivocally rejects the healthy, hockey-playing orthodoxies, 'the cult of strenuousness and self-denial', implanted by her early training.

Her contempt for the regime thrills her lover, and her eager, innocent appetite for corruption fills him with wild hope. Orwell's Julia speaks with the same voice as the Sonia who wrote in *Horizon* in 1946:

> when you have seen through [this] world you can never become its victim, but can fight it with the only unanswerable weapon – cynical despair; when you have learnt the lesson of the double vision, action and emotion are equally meaningless. This is the heritage of Catholic education . . . one which those who went to Catholic schools always recognize in each other, members of a secret society who, when they meet, huddle together, temporarily at truce with the rest of the world, while they cautiously, untrustingly, lick each other's wounds.

This is the harsh pent-up misery that made Sonia spit at nuns. Orwell's Julia talks about her own early indoctrination with the same 'open jeering hatred'. Sex is a weapon, like despair, for Julia (who sees her affair with Winston as primarily a form of resistance to the Party). It seems to have been much the same for Sonia. She would love many men, and sleep with many more but, for her, true love in its most intense and deepest form was not primarily sexual. On the two or three occasions when she broke this rule, the results were catastrophic. Orwell's portrait of Julia suggests that he understood pretty well the sort of temperament for which sex is an act of passionate defiance. For Sonia the full richness, warmth and delicacy of human feeling would find its outlet in the friendships that came in the end to occupy the centre of her life.

PART THREE

The Girl from the Fiction Department

Sonia in 1945 when Orwell took her as his model for the
heroine of Nineteen Eighty-Four

In the summer of 1946, Sonia was in Paris, turning heads among the existentialists on the Left Bank. They were dazzled by her pale, blonde English beauty, and frankly incredulous to discover that a girl in her twenties with the looks of a Hollywood film star could hold down the post of editorial assistant on the British equivalent of Jean-Paul Sartre's *Les Temps modernes*. Cyril had returned from his triumphal tour of Paris the year before with a copy of Sartre's pre-publication manifesto for that review, which would set the agenda for a whole generation of forward-looking, Leftward-leaning, idealistic Western youth. The manifesto's opening section was first published in May 1945 in a special French number of *Horizon*.

For an English readership exhausted by wartime privations, both material and moral, France and its produce – from wine, food and sunshine to art, philosophy and literature – had come to stand for civilization itself. Ten thousand copies of another *Horizon* special issue, '*La Littérature anglaise pendant la guerre*', had also been shipped across the Channel, but Connolly made no bones about the 'lassitude, brain fatigue, apathy and humdrummery of English writers'. Paris by contrast blazed with intellectual vitality and confidence. Its writers, galvanized by four humiliating years of occupation and defeat, now stood ready to ignite the torch that would light the way to freedom, choice and rational reform. *Horizon* was among the first to hand it to them. It was this symbolic handover, charged with passion on both sides, that gave Sonia from the start a romantic, semi-mythical aura in the eyes of Parisian intellectuals.

Peter Watson introduced her to Picasso's friend, Michel Leiris, an ethnographer, poet and essayist seventeen years older than herself, one of the key figures whose writings would reflect and reshape French intellectual life in the coming decades. Through Leiris she met the circle of writers, thinkers and artists – Raymond Queneau, Marguerite Duras, Jacques Lacan, Georges Bataille, André Masson – who became her friends for life. All of them (except for her near-contemporary, Marguerite Duras) belonged to an ex-surrealist generation who now looked for salvation to the Communist Party. Between them they took care of Sonia's philosophical and political education.

She reminded Leiris of a dashing and impetuous young pony, tossing her blonde mane, snuffing the cigarette-scented air on the Boulevard St Germain, pawing the ground in the Deux Magots or the Flore, always ready to rear up at the faintest hint of goad or spur in the form of a suspect or outmoded proposition. For him she would remain ever afterwards brave, loyal and true. Sonia embodied for Leiris chivalric qualities that linked her in his mind with a world of knights in armour and their trusty steeds. 'No doubt it was the innate dignity – a spontaneous dignity with nothing forced about it – of her words and gestures that made you think of the sort of pride you instinctively associate with a thoroughbred racehorse.'

Sonia also made contact with her opposite number on *Les Temps modernes*, Sartre's great friend and closest rival,

Picasso with Sonia's great friend and supporter,
the writer Michel Leiris

the philosopher Maurice Merleau-Ponty, who said he was transfixed from the first night they met by the sorrow underlying her surface gaiety. Merleau-Ponty was in his late thirties, strikingly handsome and singularly brilliant, about to become Professor of Philosophy at the Ecole Normale supérieure, and already a key figure in the moral debate currently raging about the future of democracy in France. In 1946, Sartre's *L'Etre et le néant* was generally agreed, at any rate by professional philosophers, to have been narrowly outflanked the year before by Merleau-Ponty's *La Phénoménologie de la perception*.

Merleau-Ponty was a man of immense charm and finesse. He was also, according to the writer Boris Vian, the only one of the philosophers who asked women to dance. In the days when all of them were penniless, it was Merleau-Ponty who regularly tracked down the best bands, the prettiest girls, the cheapest and most stylish bars on the Left Bank. He discovered the young Juliette Greco and impressed her by the flourish with which, at the end of an eventful evening, he handed his silver cigarette lighter to the waiter to keep until he could afford to pay the bill. Dancing became something of a touchstone for Merleau-Ponty. He took a dim view of Orwell's friend, Arthur Koestler, and clinched it in letters to Sonia by grumbling about his want of style both philosophically speaking and in person.

Koestler's girlfriend, Mamaine Paget, left a comical account of watching him lumbering round a dance floor with Simone de Beauvoir while Sartre (who had never apparently danced before) lumbered after them with Mme Albert Camus. Merleau-Ponty blamed Koestler's lack of sensuality for his dry and cerebral style of argument. He had no wit, no warmth, no grace, no sense of irony or humour, unlike another of Sonia's compatriots, A. J. Ayer (newly appointed to the chair of philosophy at University College, London), who could be forgiven anything for his elegance, high spirits and urbane resemblance to Disraeli. The two went nightclubbing together, and got on famously so long as by common consent they kept off philosophical debate.

Arthur Koestler

Merleau-Ponty wrote to Sonia that summer in correct and formal English (an effort he promptly abandoned on the grounds that he could never hope to match her perfect French), proposing an article for *Horizon* on the 'so-called humanism' of British practitioners like Orwell and Ayer. He had just completed a magisterial essay for *Les Temps modernes*, rebuking Koestler for his attacks on Stalin ('He subordinated morality to history much more ruthlessly than any existentialist yet,' Simone de Beauvoir wrote admiringly of Merleau-Ponty's defence of Soviet death camps: 'We took the leap with him'). *Horizon* turned the offer down, but Sonia herself replied at length from London on 1 July. Merleau-Ponty carried her letter about with him for nearly six months, taking it to the first post-war cultural congress at Geneva (where he was leader of the French delegation), before replying in detail to her various points about the French new novel, Koestler's pro-Jewish stance and British government policy in Palestine. He added in a courteous postscript that a word from her on less neutral topics would give him personal and, if he might say so, poetic pleasure.

He told Sonia it was the grief mixed with her gaiety that intrigued him, and made him want to see her again. He had just discovered the Tabou, a little café on the rue Dauphine that stayed open till all hours, serving coffee and croissants long after the last bar closed. Sartre, de Beauvoir and Camus followed him as regulars at a new, late-night bar that opened in the Tabou's cellar in the spring of 1947 with Juliette Greco behind the bar and Boris Vian on trumpet (the place proved an instant success, becoming such a focus of existentialist decadence in the popular imagination that it had to be closed down after twelve months). It was here that Merleau-Ponty took Sonia when she returned to Paris, moving with her through the unhurried preliminary stages of an affair like graceful practised dance steps in the spring and early summer of 1947.

They fell into the habit of meeting at one of the cafés around the church of St Germain to sit talking over coffee or Pernod, and ending the night at the Tabou, where they parted not yet with a kiss but with an even more intimate, broad, slow smile. They talked about literature and life, which meant communism, terrorism, fascism and the pre-

The philosopher Maurice Merleau-Ponty

carious future of the peace. He explained the dark side of French colonial history; she explored the implications of her childhood in British imperial India. Like Orwell before him, Merleau-Ponty was captivated by Sonia's boldness and directness, her sharp, practical intelligence, her utter indifference to the theoretical and doctrinal niceties earnestly debated in St Germain cafés at a moment when France seemed to be on the verge of disintegrating, or erupting into open war between Communists and Gaullists.

This was a time of momentous undertakings and passionate clarion calls. People flocked to Sartre, who had assumed absolute responsibility as a writer in return for unequivocal commitment. To be twenty or twenty-five at the time of the Liberation seemed, as de Beauvoir said, an immense stroke of luck. Sonia (who had been just twenty-six) enthusi-astically endorsed what she described for *Horizon*'s readers as 'the courageous, humane and astringent tradition of which Sartre has . . . been such a formidable exponent, and through which France has been willing to give so much to the world'.

But she could not entirely suppress the irreverent English irony that charmed Merleau-Ponty. She cut the ground from under his feet with what he called her sceptical socialism (or what Bill Coldstream used to call her sauciness). He said he felt the same sort of startled sympathy you might feel for a friend sidetracked in a discussion of universal ethics by a sudden craving for sweets or chocolate. Sonia had no patience with political positions that seemed to her more like childish posturing and plotting. She described for him an exasperating day spent with two fiery French socialists, the critic Roland Barthes and Dionys Mascolo from the publishing firm of Gallimard:

> *They talked about civil war as one talks about a visit to the dentist. When they came to discussing how to make efficient bombs out of bottles with petrol, I could have knocked their heads together with rage, and I only refrained from screaming when they said any form of personal pleasure was a waste of time, because they were so busy getting tight and so pleased with the clothes they had bought on the black market that it became rather touching.*

Sonia stayed in France for much of the summer, warmly encouraged by *Horizon*'s contributors and staff. Koestler urged Merleau-Ponty to find her work in Paris ('as if I needed telling,' he responded crossly). Diana Witherby cheered her on ('Enjoy yourself with Maurice, but don't be bullied in any way, will you darling'). Cyril himself instructed her not to leave before the opening of the great surrealist show in July. 'If you're madly in love & don't want to come back, say so,' he ended generously: 'we will understand.' When Merleau-Ponty finally saw her off at the Gare du Nord, Sonia blew him a kiss as the train left the station. He would return again and again to the memory of that kiss, and to an earlier parting at the Café Méphisto when she had been on the brink of tears: 'One day you must tell me a little more clearly what lies behind this despair you spoke of. I didn't dare ask at the time.'

Back in London, Sonia felt flat and stranded. She told Merleau-Ponty that each time she returned across the Channel it was as much as she could do to resume the daily office routine that left her with no energy even to imagine any other kind of life. After the ferment of Paris, bombed and burnt-out London seemed, as Cyril said, 'a grey sick wilderness on another planet'. Peter Watson saw England as a prison. All of them found it hard to bear the narrowness and insularity that closed them in at home. When the magazine moved to new premises in Bedford Square, Peter tried to cheer them up by commissioning Alberto Giacometti and his brother Diego to design and make a magnificent chandelier. He also brought his Picassos out of store to decorate the walls. 'I saw the inside of the *Horizon* office, full of horrible pictures collected by Watson,' Evelyn Waugh wrote to Nancy Mitford, '... and Miss Brownell working away with a dictionary translating some rot from the French.'

Sonia missed Parisian sophistication in the courts of love as much as in the aesthetic and intellectual arena. For her, London's Gargoyle Club was a poor substitute for the Parisian Tabou ('The tribal rites of the Gargoyle haven't changed one iota,' she wrote glumly that winter to Peter's American boyfriend, Waldemar Hansen, in New York). Spender tells a nice story about Sonia at the Gargoyle with Sartre and Simone de Beauvoir, who was entertaining the other two with an authoritative analysis of what was wrong with Englishmen, when Lucian Freud walked in. According to Sonia, de Beauvoir immediately changed her mind, and shortly afterwards left the club with him. Bacon's friend Dan Farson told the same story, only this time it was Sartre who revised his opinion in Freud's favour.

At all events, Sonia agreed with both of them. The rituals of a formal French courtship made it harder than ever to take the usual homegrown tactics of pounce and grab. At some point after the war, she had undergone an abortion, convalescing afterwards with Cyril in Brighton. Sonia said the father of the child was Arthur Koestler whom she never liked, and whom she described long afterwards as a sadist. She seems to have confided in no more than three people, and it is a measure of her faith in Maurice Merleau-Ponty that she told him directly or by implication what had happened. Presumably this episode explains the acid references in his letters to Koestler's vanity, and clumsiness with women.

Maurice told Sonia she gave him confidence and strength of purpose. He said she took him out of the endless competitive jockeying and jostling for advantage among political and intellectual factions in Paris. Under her influence he

Man at Night, *self-portrait by Lucian Freud*

could work calmly at saner and more satisfying subjects like poetry and philosophy. They made plans to meet that autumn. Having failed to find her a job in Paris, Maurice followed her instead to London, arriving with two or three French friends who were charmed, as he was, by the delights

Sonia laid on for them in London, Oxford and Cambridge. When she sent him a letter afterwards full of the despair that had struck him so forcibly at their first meeting in Paris, it only sharpened his determination to spend more time with her in England.

He asked her to sound out Freddy Ayer, now running the philosophy department at University College with characteristic bravura, about the possibility of fixing him up with some academic teaching. In the meantime he set about improving his English by filling in the questionnaires in a manual called *Meet Yourself*. The one he liked best diagnosed him as the kind of man who advances towards love with a knife gripped between his teeth. It was a style that suited Sonia. 'I never longed for anything in my life so much as M,' she wrote later in a rare scrap of reminiscence jotted down on a blank page in one of George's notebooks. Maurice returned to London for a week after Christmas, catching the boat-train on Boxing Day 1947 and telegraphing Sonia to meet him at Victoria. They finally became lovers in her flat on Percy Street, where they saw the New Year in together.

He had always wanted to see Sonia at home, in her own context – 'performing your own behaviour,' as he put it – surrounded by her friends and talking animatedly in English. They explored Fitzrovia and Soho, dining the night before he left at the White Tower in high good humour with themselves and one another. Maurice vividly remembered Sonia's contentment at this meal together, her gaiety and vitality, the honesty and lack of pretence with which she talked about herself and her family. One of the things he liked best about her was her Englishness.

The qualities that made London seem so dull, stuffy and hopelessly backward-looking to restive spirits like Sonia were delightful to Maurice. He loved the poise and style of English manners. The politeness that seemed to her to cloak the simplest transaction under a veneer of insincerity struck him as an elaborate code of civility and restraint which he hoped would rub off on him when he got back to France. The waistcoat Sonia bought him for Christmas became a kind of talisman: he liked the dandified London air it gave him, and the old-fashioned English courtesy that went with it.

Maurice returned without enthusiasm to the mayhem simmering on the streets of Paris. He wrote to Sonia a few days after he got back, wearily reporting various New Year celebrations, communist and anti-communist, that had degenerated into the usual acrimonious squabbling. He described the novelist Raymond Queneau, dead drunk and on top form, pursuing a couple of tarts at a party, while Roland Barthes collected a black eye at another. Maurice himself ended up on the Metro in the small hours involved in a rough-house with the police. He was too fastidious to enjoy this kind of dust-up. At the same time he was too passionately involved in political dialectic to be able to stand aloof, like Camus, whose charm, gentleness and proven courage as a Resistance hero set him apart as, in Sonia's words, 'the Galahad of the left-wing intellectuals'.

Of all the Knights of the Round Table, Sir Galahad was the youngest and purest, morally and sexually the most nearly stainless. Maurice Merleau-Ponty was no Galahad. He was expert at the subtle, insidious, perhaps unconscious accommodations that enabled so many Frenchmen to transfer or extend allegiance wholesale from the Catholic church to the Communist Party. He told Sonia he had seldom felt so close to Sartre as when his old friend assured him that, if it came to open war, he would fight with the Communists unless the Soviet Union intervened (Russian troops, massing in Eastern Europe, would seize Czechoslovakia that spring and blockade Berlin).

He also had a wife and child. Sonia said Maurice taught her much about both herself and him. One of the first things she had to learn was to accept in theory if not in practice the difference – so difficult for even an English cradle Catholic to grasp – between love and *un amour* ('the fact that these two words are not an exact translation of each other,' she wrote in retrospect, 'has caused more confusion between the English and the French than most of the wars of politics and religion'). Like Sartre and de Beauvoir, Maurice and his wife had negotiated a modern variation on the traditional French Catholic etiquette that distinguishes sharply between wife and mistress, while firmly discouraging any attempt to confuse the roles. If Sonia was to be his titular mistress, she must see that she could not also be his wife.

Maurice noted another difference of approach underlying his longing to be quietly back with her in London, and Sonia's to be at his side in tumultuous Paris. His admiration for everything cool, calm and balanced in English society collided with the instinct that drew her to the violence and instability currently unleashed in France. Her taste for danger both disturbed and attracted him. He suspected – as many others would do after him – that there were at least two different Sonias. The one who enchanted him was the comical, saucy, reckless Sonia who could down three cocktails in half an hour, the Sonia whose frankness startled her lover and made him laugh, whose warmth and delicacy touched his heart, the Sonia who seemed – as he said, quoting Stendhal – to be made for happiness:

> *This is the one to whom I said in Paris: You can't know how you look, the one who loves Apollinaire, the one who blew me a kiss through the train window on leaving Paris, above all the one who, lying on her bed last Friday night, touched my back so gently and called me darling.*

This was the Sonia who bewitched others all her life, and whose abrupt disappearance invariably came as a shock. Maurice didn't care for the second self who replaced the first, the wary, reticent Sonia whose uncertainty made her overbearing, the Sonia who could never trust herself or anyone else, especially not someone who seemed in retrospect to have surprised her into an intimacy she feared and could not sustain.

Things had gone badly wrong between Sonia and Merleau-Ponty towards the end of their last night in London, when they had talked for hours in a long, intimate, interrogatory exchange that ended in tears and painful self-exposure. They turned away from one another in mutual hostility and distress. Next morning she served him breakfast with a determined cheerfulness that held him implacably at arm's length. She slammed doors and clashed plates. He recognized in her a harsh, barely suppressed anger that lasted until they reached the station where, as he climbed on board the train, she bent her head and hid behind the curtain of her hair in a parting gesture that once again touched him deeply.

But he must have known that the angry Sonia, suddenly let loose like a genie from a bottle, had a raging destructive energy that could never be entirely contained. Merleau-Ponty had precipitated the release of a similar genie once before. He had been a student, not yet twenty years old, when he first met Simone de Beauvoir (the two of them, with Simone Weill, had come top in philosophy in the national examinations of 1927), and fell in love with her best friend, who loved him in return. The pair seemed ideally matched to everyone except her rigidly conventional, Catholic bourgeois family, who put a brutal stop to the affair. The girl, crushed between irreconcilable opposing forces, lost her emotional balance, spiralling downwards over a few days into fever, delirium and death.

De Beauvoir told the story in her *Memoirs of a Dutiful Daughter* (where Maurice Merleau-Ponty is renamed Jean Pradelle), explaining in her last sentence that she felt she had bought her own freedom at the expense of the friend who had paid in some sense with her life. 'A useless, heartless tragedy,' wrote Sonia, reviewing the book, 'which makes one detest the society which could produce it.' She found de Beauvoir often humourless, turgid and over-solemn. But she admired from the bottom of her heart the robust determination underlying the hugely successful public and private career that had seemed inconceivable at the outset for any girl of de Beauvoir's generation. There was little Sonia herself did not know about the guilt that had destroyed Merleau-Ponty's first love: the guilt of children who fail to please their parents, of Catholic daughters rejected by the Church, of girls unable to comply with social pressures that denied them any right to independent choice or action.

Maurice remained perplexed, as many others would be after him, by the intensity of her desperation, and by her fatalistic sense that there was nothing to be done about it. Their mutual attraction grew more urgent. Sonia said, at the time and ever afterwards, that Maurice Merleau-Ponty was the love of her life. He sent her another quotation that had leaped out at him from the pages of Stendhal's *Le Rouge et le noir*, about giving oneself up to love, being overcome by love as by fever or morphine. He ended one of his long, troubled, hair-splitting letters, festooned by doubts and cavils that he knew would give her more pain than pleasure, with what was perhaps as far as a philosophical phenomenologist could go towards a simple declaration: 'May I say something out of order? . . . Well, here goes: I see your position, and I love it. M.'

Sonia joined him in Paris in the spring of 1948. There were more meetings at newly discovered, convivial little cafés, more nights together at her hotel on the rue Jacob, more of the outbursts that always made him smile when her long, shapely English sentences rose to an energetic crescendo of despair followed by an abrupt demand for a double Pernod. He planned to take her south for the first time to show her Aix and Avignon.

The trouble between them was still her nostalgia for the absolute, the legacy from a Catholic childhood that Sonia saw as 'the cancer at the heart of so many disastrous love affairs'. Maurice was puzzled by her insistence from the start that their love for one another was inextricably linked to suffering and sorrow. He baffled her in turn by simultaneously testing her faith in him ('I can't live with a woman who isn't jealous of me'), proclaiming his confidence in her and protesting vehemently if she looked at another man. His probing, analytical mind rode emotion like a well-schooled horse. She struggled to dismiss her jealousy as a physical symptom ('secondary like the toothache'), and to treat her longing for a more absolute commitment as a pernicious aberration:

> It is also Perfectionism, the belief in Romantic Love, in 'Mr Right' etc., but above all it is the inability to accept anything imperfect ie human in the person one loves which on the reverse side of the coin is an inability to accept the limitations of one's own personality.

However much she hoped he might marry her, there was no question of Maurice divorcing his wife. The upshot was that Sonia returned to Paris, probably in the latter part of 1948 or the following spring, to find him gone. She had been held up by Cyril at the *Horizon* office in London. When she reached the Hôtel Jacob, there was a note waiting for her from Mme Merleau-Ponty, returning Sonia's letter to her husband, explaining that he had left town, and suggesting a meeting. 'You must be cursing Cyril for not letting you go sooner,' Diana wrote in answer to a distracted postcard from Paris, 'and us for saying he would still be there! . . . I'm sure Maurice will come back to see you – or is it an end?'

It was the end. There would be more meetings, and at least one attempt at reconciliation, but these encounters came to nothing. Twenty years later Sonia conveyed the shock of that loss to another, much younger Frenchman, who said he had never seen anything like her absolute desolation and incomprehension. 'I had the impression of a lost child. She couldn't understand what had happened. She kept repeating: "Why did he love me? *And why did he stop loving me?*" She had a face of surprise and horror still.'

Sonia plunged back into work. For long stretches of 1949 she was fully occupied at *Horizon* in the absence of both editors. Peter was away for the first four months of the year in the US, where he broke off relations with one lover, returning to spend the summer on the continent with another. In London, he devoted more and more of his attention and resources to helping to found the Institute of Contemporary Arts. Cyril, too, steadily lost interest in the daily running of the magazine, becoming increasingly preoccupied with projects of his own and distracted by an unsatisfactory love life. First-hand experience made Sonia an infinitely sympathetic confidante to jilted or abandoned lovers ('I think we ought to drop all this nonsense about a Review of Art and Literature,' she wrote briskly to Peter's former boyfriend, 'and call it straight out "Advice to the Lovelorn" ').

Peter, always sensitive and supportive where Sonia was concerned, took her with him in July on the first leg of his travels. She stayed in Paris just long enough for what proved to be a dismal confirmation that things were over between herself and Merleau-Ponty. He told her his one regret was that he had never had a chance to fill her in on Gestalt theory, always one of his great strengths as a philosopher. Sonia came back to London alone to stand in for Cyril, who had himself left for France in early June, and would not return until mid September. By that time Sonia had agreed to marry George Orwell.

Nineteen Eighty-Four came out that summer in England

George Orwell

and America to immediate acclaim ('with cries of terror rising above the applause,' noted the *New York Times Book Review*). Orwell had worked steadily on the novel, breaking off only when forced to do so by increasingly severe tubercular crises, throughout the entire course of Sonia's affair with Merleau-Ponty. He had sketched out a first draft on Jura in the summer of 1946, returning to the island to continue work the following April with a bottle of brandy supplied by Sonia. He wrote to her two days after his arrival to say how much he longed for her to join him, enclosing detailed instructions (she was to bring a raincoat, stout boots and iron rations), and ending with a flash of the rare gentleness that contrasted so sharply with Orwell's studiously dry and offhand style: 'take care of yourself & be happy.'

In fact they did not meet again for almost two years, an interval that became a race between the completion of Orwell's novel and the collapse of his health. Memories of Sonia – her youth and prettiness, her toughness, above all her radiant vitality – fed directly into the book's heroine (who puts in a sixty-hour week or more tending the literary machines in the offices of the Fiction Department at the Ministry of Truth). Sonia's imagined presence kept company with Orwell on the island as Julia's comforted his hero, Winston:

> *She was very young, he thought, she still expected something from life . . . She would not accept it as a law of nature that the individual is always defeated . . . All you needed was luck and cunning and boldness. She did not understand that there is no such thing as happiness, that the only victory lay in the far future, long after you were dead.*

Orwell's own rapidly worsening condition enriched and deepened the novel's visionary power. He relieved what might have been an almost unbearable bleakness with muffled jokes at his own expense as a lover in his account of Winston's physical clumsiness, and the strange proposal he makes to Julia ('I'm 39 years old . . . I've got varicose veins. I've got five false teeth'), which echoes the strictly practical grounds on which the author had himself once suggested marriage to three or four successive girls, including Sonia.

When they next met, Orwell was dying. He had completed *Nineteen Eighty-Four* on Jura, posting the typescript to his publishers at the end of 1948, and almost immediately following it south himself to enter the sanatorium in Gloucestershire where Sonia visited him throughout the spring and summer. In these months when the doctors forbade him to work, when he was sometimes almost too weak to hold a pen, when his skeletal frailty and waxen pallor shocked his friends, his mind remained active, lucid and humane. Literary contacts, basic secretarial services, help with postage and typing came from Sonia. 'She helped her friends in need as if she, herself, had no need of help,' wrote David Plante, who understood better than most the gnawing self-doubt that made Sonia acutely sensitive to misery in others.

George and Sonia had both suffered, and changed, a great deal in the three years since their original abortive affair. Both now desperately needed consolation. Orwell recognized the emotional vulnerability and the stubborn, unworldly moral sense that underlay Sonia's surface cynicism. In one of his last reviews he restated the view of friendship Sonia had herself expressed far more clumsily a few years earlier in *Horizon*, when she struggled to pin down what was wrong with the perfectionist's craving for the absolute. Orwell defined the essence of ordinary human love in a discussion of Mahatma Gandhi's claim that, as a good Hindu, he would see his wife and child starve sooner than give them chicken broth:

> *This attitude is perhaps a noble one, but . . . it is inhuman. The essence of being human is that one does not seek perfection, that one is sometimes willing to commit sins for the sake of loyalty,*

that one does not push asceticism to the point where it makes friendly intercourse impossible, and that one is prepared in the end to be defeated and broken up by life, which is the inevitable price of fastening one's love upon other human individuals. No doubt alcohol, tobacco and so forth are things that a saint must avoid, but . . . Many people genuinely do not wish to be saints, and it is probable that some who achieve or aspire to sainthood have never felt much temptation to be human beings.

The ironic tone of this passage, with its undertow of strong feeling, might almost be Sonia speaking. She was no saint, nor was she ever remotely tempted to avoid alcohol, tobacco and so forth. A fair number of her mistakes, even more of her misfortunes, came precisely from taking loyalty too far. She would be defeated and broken up by life, as Orwell must have known he was about to be when he wrote these words. For most of his life, ideas had mattered more to him than people. 'He was interested in ideas, and really believed that people were governed in their behaviour by them,' Sonia wrote later, 'hence the failure of his relationships with women which never taught him anything but always left him confused, wounded, and according to his very sincere beliefs the injured party.'

Men who loved ideas held an irresistible allure for Sonia, who had no faith in her own worth or talents but responded unconditionally to creative drive and intellectual originality in others. When Orwell reached out at the end, he found an answering sweetness and strength in her. The pact between them grew from mutual honesty, humour and compassion. 'Her marrying Orwell had to do with her own deep unhappiness,' wrote Ian Angus (Sonia's close friend and co-editor on Orwell's *Collected Essays*), 'and the recognition by an unhappy man that she was deeply unhappy.'

Orwell, who knew that the most he could count on was a few more years as a semi-invalid, hoped to salvage time to write from the wreckage of his life. His approach was forthright and anti-romantic. Sonia recalled his exact words for Ian long afterwards: 'for the record – when he proposed to me – *learn how to make dumplings.*' George's wry, dry, minimalist proposal stirred the passionate protective generosity at the root of Sonia's being. She made no pretence of being in love with him and, at any rate to start with, acknowledged his need of her far more readily than hers of him. 'He said he would get better if I married him,' she told me twenty years later, 'so, you see, I had no choice.'

Orwell said the same at the time to his publisher and others. His closest friends longed, as he did, to believe it. Koestler, as fond of George as he was ambivalent about Sonia, wrote to say it was the best thing that could have happened to either of them. Others felt less sanguine. Peter Watson was dubious, Cyril outraged, Olivier Popham positively shocked by news of the engagement. In September George was moved to University College Hospital in Gower Street, where Sonia married him at his bedside on 13 October. The witnesses were George's old ally, the newspaper proprietor David Astor, and Sonia's friend Janetta (then married to Robert Kee) from *Horizon*, who found the simple ceremony extremely moving.

Visitors to his sickbed that autumn all agreed that Sonia (like Julia) brought warmth and comfort to the last months of her lover's life. 'Whenever she arrived . . . bringing literary gossip, she seemed to light up the hospital room in which Orwell lay with her vivacity and laughter,' wrote Tosco Fyvel: 'I thought that Orwell desperately looked forward to her coming.' 'In spite of the tragic circumstances . . . marriage immensely cheered him,' wrote Anthony Powell, who visited the hospital most days and found his friend's 'old Wodehousian side' beginning to flicker up again: 'in some respects he was on better form there than I had ever known him show.'

Orwell's visitors were allowed to stay for twenty minutes each for fear of tiring him. Sonia spent an hour with him every day. Stephen Spender (who came only twice) was dismayed by Sonia's bossiness and impatience when the two men discussed politics. But Spender's wife, Natasha, watched George glancing affectionately at Sonia during this interchange: 'He knew perfectly well how bored she was, and it amused him. He understood her brusque and nervy moments, he knew the illness made her anxious.' The couple developed a teasing, sparring manner that suited the prickliness each habitually employed to cloak or check any uprush of deep feeling.

Their plan was for Sonia to leave her job (*Horizon*, which had been facing closure for some time, would shut down altogether three months after her marriage), and go with George to a sanatorium in the Swiss Alps, where his doctor thought there might be some chance of stabilizing his condition as a chronic invalid. All parties agreed that his five-year-old son Richard – who had been looked after on Jura by George's sister for more than half his life – would remain in his aunt's care. George reckoned that royalties from his latest book should be sufficient to meet the child's needs, settle his hospital bills, and cover travel and other

*Sonia (with Lys Lubbock) on her last
day at* Horizon

expenses for himself, his wife and her friend, Lucian Freud,
who was to help with lifting and carrying on the journey.

George died of a lung haemorrhage on 21 January 1950,
four days before they were due to fly to Switzerland. 'Sonia
came to see us the same evening,' wrote George's old
friend, the journalist Malcolm Muggeridge: 'She cried and
cried. I shall always love her for her true tears on that
occasion.' She blamed herself for not having been at his
bedside. The hospital had failed to reach her in time because
Lucian and his current girlfriend, the painter Anne Dunn,
had invited her to discuss last-minute travel arrangements
at a little bar across the street from her flat in an attempt to
cheer her up.

'Malcolm's description of her grief was a moderate one,' said Natasha, who spent a whole afternoon weeks later with Sonia convulsed by storms of weeping: 'She really did believe she was going to save George's life. She believed he would get better in Switzerland, and she talked about how she was going to look after him when they got back. When he died, it was cataclysmic. She had persuaded herself she loved him intellectually, for his writing, but she found she *really* loved him.' Natasha felt that part of the shock for Sonia, who thought she had married George for the noblest and most disinterested reasons, was that his death brought home to her too late the depth of her own emotional involvement.

Sonia described later to Ian Angus the married future she had planned with George to revolve around his need to work. He would rest and write in his pyjamas while she dealt with his correspondence, organized his literary affairs, entertained their friends and looked in on him at intervals with delicious things to eat and drink. The role of literary handmaid was one she felt herself born to play. 'Her heart was set on it,' said Natasha. But Sonia hadn't bargained on how desperately she missed George's physical presence. The intensity of this second loss was still vivid to her more than twenty years later when she wrote to comfort the actress Jill Balcon, after the death of her own husband, the poet laureate, Cecil Day Lewis. Jill replied that no one had grasped her predicament so accurately as Sonia:

Who knows better than you how totally unanchored one feels? No amount of foreknowledge protects one from the terrible, final, stunning shock. Who knows better than you how much closer

one is to someone so dear who needs nursing for months and
months? You know it all, poor Sonia.

George had stipulated a church burial, but Sonia was for once in no fit state to organize anything. All the arrangements were made by Muggeridge and Powell, who chose to read the biblical passage about the breaking of the golden bowl. 'The lesson was from Ecclesiastes, the grinders in the street, the grasshopper a burden, the silver cord loosed, the wheel broken at the cistern,' Powell wrote in his memoirs: 'For some reason George Orwell's funeral service was one of the most harrowing I have ever attended.'

In a will drawn up three days before he died, Orwell had entrusted his literary estate to Sonia, who was his sole heir. In the previous few months, she had already taken over the day-to-day running of his career. Long afterwards, when she came to work on the four volumes of his collected writings, she talked to Ian Angus about these months when George discussed his work with her, and what he wanted done with it. Under the terms of his will, George made Sonia directly responsible for enforcing his determination that there should be no biography. He gave her no warning beforehand about this provision, which would cause more trouble than anything else in the whole document.

But he did discuss with her his wish to include a clause calling for the suppression of his early novels which Sonia, with support from his friends and from his publisher Fred Warburg, persuaded him to drop. Orwell died dissatisfied with his output, feeling that he had wasted too much time on ephemeral journalism. He told Sonia (who told Ian

Angus) that he had two more novels in him waiting to be written. Sonia had watched him stubbornly resist editorial changes to the typescript of *Nineteen Eighty-Four*, and he knew he could depend on her to safeguard the future of his work with an austerity that matched his own.

He had already regularized the business side of his affairs by handing over their management in 1947 to a company – George Orwell Productions Ltd – set up for tax purposes by his accountants, Harrison, Son, Hill & Co. 'Around the time of our marriage, George told me that he understood absolutely nothing about money or tax problems,' wrote Sonia, who never questioned her husband's advice that money matters were best left to Harrison Hill's senior partner, Jack Harrison. 'When George died Jack Harrison . . . made a great declaration to me, saying he would always look after me, would see to all financial problems, and that I was not to worry. I was very touched by this declaration, and very grateful for the help he offered.'

At two board meetings convened in the hospital on 23 November 1949 and 17 January 1950, Harrison had become a director of George Orwell Productions Ltd, and owner of one share. The other two directors were Mr and Mrs Eric Blair. 'Eric Blair' had been Orwell's name until he took a pseudonym as a writer, and switched identities so completely that even his old schoolfriends had to learn to call him George. Both his wives were officially 'Mrs Blair', and his adopted son remained ever afterwards Richard Blair, so as to retain the same name as the aunt who brought him up, George's sister, Avril Blair. But, by the time of his second marriage, George himself had long since rejected the name of Blair for all but legal purposes. Like everyone else who met him in the 1940s, Sonia never knew him as anything but George Orwell.

On Harrison's advice, George had arranged for his literary agents to pay all royalties directly to the company. Sonia, who had initially owned a single share, inherited all the rest under the terms of his will. From now on she would pay her own earnings over to George Orwell Productions, and receive in return an annual stipend of £500, leaving the rest to build up reserves for Richard's future. 'George Orwell is dead, and Mrs Orwell presumably a rich widow,' wrote Evelyn Waugh, who might have been glad to know that Orwell's entire estate was officially assessed for probate at just under £10,000. For the greater part of his professional career, his income had never amounted to more than a few hundred pounds a year.

He had consulted an accountant (on the advice of his friend, the writer Jon Kimche) when he found himself liable to pay income tax for the first time in his life with the success of *Animal Farm*, after which his income once more dropped back sharply. It rose again with *Nineteen Eighty-Four*, but the most Orwell himself anticipated at this stage was 'at any rate a small income from royalties for some years to come' (his exact estimate was £11,970 over the next five years). The situation would change only after his death, with the paperback publication of *Animal Farm* and *Nineteen Eighty-Four*.

For all his rising reputation, in 1949 Orwell was no great catch from a commercial or literary point of view. 'He was a dry old stick,' said Vera Russell, one of many who wrote him off in his lifetime, and became increasingly exasperated by the fuss made about him afterwards: 'No one thought twice about him at the time. One had Eliot in one's life, and Auden – one played *The Wasteland* on the gramophone – and one wouldn't have *dreamed* of putting Orwell in the same class as Aldous Huxley.' The fact is that Sonia put him in the top class as a writer well ahead of his more fashion-conscious peers, and long before the popular readership that would turn Orwell's work into a force to reckon with, and transpose his life into the realm of myth.

Many of Orwell's oldest friends, who had been taken aback to find her running his affairs in the last months of his life, were even more disconcerted to discover that he had left her in charge of his literary estate. Sonia would earn considerable ill feeling from male contemporaries who felt themselves better qualified than she was to say what might be best for his reputation. Prospective biographers found her objection to their plans inappropriate and overbearing. She responded to a rising tide of discontent in 1955 by announcing the appointment of Malcolm Muggeridge as official biographer (Muggeridge had promised to do nothing further about the project, and he never did). To the end of her life Sonia stuck resolutely to the spirit of her husband's will. Orwell had trusted her literary judgement, respected her efficiency, and relied on her obstinacy to prevent his work being what he called 'mucked about' by posterity. Neither he nor she could have foreseen that his charge would eventually destroy her.

Over the years, Sonia would lay herself open by proxy to what Powell called the tactics of smear and boycott employed by the orthodox left wing to discredit Orwell's uncompromising stance on Soviet totalitarianism. In 1949 her Parisian friends had learned with dismay that she had married a figure whose reputation as an arch anti-Stalinist was already beginning to filter through to France. But they responded warmly to her distress when the end came. Friends on both sides of the Channel urged her to get away, to leave London, to put space and time between herself and the harrowing memory of George's disintegration and death.

Sonia left for Paris in March. Like many people who fail to give or get satisfaction in their own families, she looked elsewhere for support and affection. She said she felt in Paris as if she belonged to a large, convivial, adoptive family that met every morning over coffee in one or other café to swap news, catch up on gossip, compare notes or commiserate about the night before. Now her French friends rallied round, providing consolation, distraction, the loan of flats, and invitations for the holidays. Even Merleau-Ponty revived his old plan to take her south to Provence, to visit the ruins of les Baux and explore the Mediterranean coast. They had got as far as St Tropez when Sonia wrote to Cyril to say they had quarrelled again, and parted for good. She found refuge with the writer Georges Bataille and his wife.

For the next ten years and more, Sonia would divide her time between London and Paris. Her services were promptly snapped up by ambitious publishers starting up again after the war. The first was Albert Skira in Geneva, who knew her from joint art-publishing ventures arranged by Peter Watson with *Horizon*. In 1951 it was George Weidenfeld who secured her first as reader, then editor, for his newly founded firm of Weidenfeld and Nicolson. Weidenfeld, who by his own account knew little about novels at this stage, relied on Sonia to lay the foundations of his fiction list. In the next five years she brought him singular success with Nigel Dennis, Sybille Bedford and Dan Jacobsen as well as a whole constellation of Americans: Saul Bellow, Mary McCarthy, Elizabeth Hardwick and Norman Mailer.

She made translations for her French circle, especially for Leiris and for Marguerite Duras, who became perhaps the closest of her woman friends in the 1950s. In these years when Duras's reputation as novelist, playwright and screenwriter went from strength to strength in France and beyond, Sonia toyed with the idea of writing a novel herself. 'How would it go?' she asked herself, listing her heroine's problems as her looks, her love affairs, her moral courage. 'The real problem is – dependence – sexual? financial? Power – children.'

The novel (which never apparently got beyond a rough draft) sounds much like other fictional attempts by Sonia's friends – Duras herself, Mary McCarthy, Edna O'Brien – to explore the position of the second sex at a time when it was changing faster and more drastically than probably at any previous period in history. Simone de Beauvoir's *The Mandarins* (which won her the Prix Goncourt in 1954) was a thinly disguised version of recent interchanges between herself and Sartre, Merleau-Ponty, Camus, Koestler and others. Some said she put Sonia in it too. In fact it was Marguerite Duras who included an unmistakable portrait of Sonia in her fifth novel, *Les Petits Chevaux de Tarquinie*.

The two had spent the summer of 1952 together at Bocca di Magra on the Italian coast with Marguerite's current lover, Dionys Mascolo, and two Italian friends, the philosopher Elio Vittorini and his wife Ginetta. In the book written up at top speed immediately afterwards by Marguerite, both couples are on the verge of splitting up. They pass long, hot, aimless days swimming, eating, dancing, sleeping and talking together under the dispassionate and observant eye of an English beauty called Diana, whose sole companion is her glass of bitter Campari ('I know readers who became addicted to that treacherous, blood-red drink,' wrote Duras' biographer, 'after reading *Les Petits Chevaux de Tarquinie*').

Sonia in Italy, modelling for a novel
by Marguerite Duras

The novel is a direct transcript of reality (so much so as to be unpublishable, according to the author's friends, whose unanimous opposition failed to prevent its coming out the following September). Through all her companions' permutations of boredom and desire, Diana remains unattached and unattainable, neither predatory nor prey. She has Sonia's style, sharpness and wit as well as the inconsolable unhappiness that makes her friends feel by turns troubled and impatient. All agree that, however dismal anyone else may feel, none of them can match Diana's sadness. Her sombre self-knowledge cuts like a refrain through the others' desultory attempts to divert themselves and her by fixing her up with a lover:

> *All I can say, said Diana, is that up till now I've only ever slept with men whose ideas were clear, and it has never worked for me. They were always men who knew nothing of the import or meaning of love . . . In the end literature can be as fatal as anything else, you can't get over it . . . it's true that, for me, intelligence is an obsession like any other.*

This is the Sonia whose melancholy sparkled, according to the novelist Georges Limbour, like a crisp white wine. Limbour told Sonia he preferred to stick to gloomy, sweet white wines when drinking alone because a dry white reminded him too vividly of her gaiety, and her absence. He tried to tempt her back to Paris with a series of choice bottles – a fine local brandy, a fierce marc from the Côte d'Azur – setting them up in his flat like statues to represent her presence, and mimic her forceful, accusatory or revelatory gestures. He was mystified by the way his writing, in her English translation, somehow took on the airy tossing motion of her hair. From time to time Limbour and others crossed the Channel to rout her out. 'Everybody longs to see you . . .' he wrote: 'the echo of your laugh in my heart silences all the echoes of Paris.'

From now on Sonia found herself pursued by a chorus of entreaty, indignation, regrets, even menaces from French friends who felt she spent altogether too much time in London. The psychoanalyst Jacques Lacan visited her more than once ('Dearest Sonia, what a pleasure it always is to see you again! Your welcome is as warm every time as if you'd been warned of one's coming the day before'). Janine Queneau and the Batailles begged her to return to France. Marguerite, who missed her dreadfully, offered the loan of her flat. When that didn't work, she threatened to add to Sonia's problems by buying her a little flat of her own round the corner from St Germain des Prés, and furnishing it with a bed, a lamp and an ashtray ('so you'd say: "Now I'll have to come to Paris to see about that wretched flat"').

Sonia's one serious affair in these years was with the American photographer, John Phillips, who restored her confidence and sense of balance. Their relationship, built round his assignments for *Life* magazine in Paris, was warm, affectionate and relaxed. Sonia's only complaint was that living with someone who liked regular hot meals played havoc with her habitual routines. Her frequent disappearances throughout the 1950s gave rise to much grumbling and ribald speculation in London as in Paris. People on both sides of the Channel felt she was about to give them the slip. 'The first port of call of any woman friend of hers who's left her husband is Sonia's spare bed,' Cyril said in a much-quoted aphorism.

Soon he needed to put into port himself. Sonia had roped him in as literary mentor to George Weidenfeld, who published the anthology Cyril dedicated to her, *The Golden*

Marguerite Duras at the time when she and Sonia became best friends

Horizon, in 1953, and followed it up by falling in love with Cyril's wife. In the long, complex series of confrontations and conflagrations that followed – as Barbara Connolly successively eloped with, divorced, married and offered to remarry her husband and lover – Sonia became Cyril's prime confidante and go-between. He compared his rival to a rapacious giant or malevolent dwarf from Wagner's *Rheingold*. Barbara herself said that the Rhine maidens at Covent Garden reminded her of 'a chorus of Sonia Orwells'. Cyril threatened suicide ('I don't know whether to kill him or myself,' he wrote, prudently instructing Sonia to help herself to £50 from his Weidenfeld royalty account in the event of the latter option). Sonia loaned him her flat in Percy Street as a base for wooing Barbara back (she complained the bed was lumpy), and interceded energetically on his behalf with her employer.

Sonia told Edmund Wilson in 1956 that she had fled England to get away from Cyril, whose importunate phone calls as soon as she got back made her want to leave again immediately. In the end she decided the only thing to do was to hand her resignation to Weidenfeld. 'You are very cold & stern, with white face,' Cyril wrote, picturing the scene with relish: '& W mops and mows & puts on his wailing wall expression . . . And it is the beginning of the disasters that overtake the cardboard Hagen . . . I think I just pull through but probably lose my job as well as wife, home etc. . . . A rosy future for you in another country . . . I wonder what your big change can be?'

It seems to have been Peter Watson who prompted Sonia to review her life at this point. She had loved, trusted and looked up to him for years. He stood in for the affectionate, understanding elder brother she had never had, teasing and spoiling her, giving her good advice, following her exploits with an amused and attentive eye. The two saw much of one another in Paris in the early 1950s, when she was chronically hard up on her modest salary from Weidenfeld channelled through George Orwell Productions. Footloose himself, Peter watched her becoming increasingly rootless and restless, prevented by government restrictions from earning money in France, and struggling to retain a London base.

Sonia's flat may have been small and shabby, but it was inviting and hospitable, like all the homes she ever had. It was big enough to work in, and to entertain or shelter friends. Once she took in the American writers, Jane and

Paul Bowles, who made the place their own, lounging about all day as Paul wrote ruefully afterwards, without Sonia ever showing the faintest sign of impatience or dismay. 'Percy Street was her nest,' said James Lord. Peter Watson knew how important it was for her to have a place to call her own.

Peter's home life was in its way as operatic as Cyril's. On 7 May 1956, after a row with his then boyfriend, he was found drowned in his bath in his Bayswater apartment. The coroner's verdict was accidental death. 'We still feel as if the thing couldn't have happened, we just can't believe it,' Graham Sutherland wrote gently to Sonia in Paris the day after the inquest. His letter reached her too late for the funeral, but she returned to pay her last respects to Peter by taking charge of the remnants of his life, comforting his friend, clearing out his flat, and overseeing the sale of his collection.

She threw up her job that summer on the strength of a legacy of £2,000, Peter's parting gift. James Bond's creator, Ian Fleming, snapped her up on a three-month contract for the *Sunday Times*, posting her as a first assignment to Jerusalem in late August 1956, as the Suez Canal crisis moved towards its climax. Sonia's passionate sympathy for the Jewish people went back to the early formative influence of Eugene Vinaver (whose Polish family had disappeared into the Warsaw ghetto, and perished in Treblinka). Her Jerusalem dispatches centred on the future to be shaped by her own contemporaries, the young farmers, workers and fighters who held the future of Israel in their hands.

Her response was fiercely partisan. The original pioneers – 'philosopher-statesmen, serious, erudite, conscious of great tasks' – had given way to a buccaneering generation under a commander-in-chief, General Moshe Dayan, whose courage and conviction were as captivating as his black eye-patch, his archaeological expertise and his love of the arts. Sonia described Dayan and his peers as proud, brave, hot-tempered, clear-sighted, irreverent and hedonistic. They were in short everything she most admired. She fell under the spell of the most popular of them all, the hero of the War of Independence, General Yigal Allon, who was said to have asked nonchalantly, in the telegram reporting his defeat of Egypt in 1948: 'What shall I do next?' He and Sonia had just time for a brief, intense wartime affair before she returned to London at the end of September, leaving her Israeli friends to invade Egypt again while the British bombed the canal zone.

Marguerite and her French contemporaries would see to it that Sonia fought at their side in the cafés and meeting halls of Paris in the later part of the decade, when the Algerian war looked at times as if it might engulf the mainland. Her support for freedom fighters, outsiders, underdogs, anyone underprivileged or in revolt against authority was unquestioning and instinctive. Her impact could be stunning ('I've been asked out by the King of Mauritius,' she wrote breezily to Leiris from Douglas Cooper's castle of Castille, where she was attending an African festival in 1957, 'but I preferred to accept the Chief of the Tuaregs').

Fleming wanted her to move to Paris and become a monthly columnist – 'a sort of Nancy Orwell or Sonia Mitford' – reporting from the Left Bank on a year's trial basis. But Sonia's gifts were editorial rather than journalistic.

The arrangement lapsed, although she continued to write intermittently for the London press and to translate for her French friends (it was Sonia who made the English versions of Duras's two highly successful plays, *Days in the Trees* and *The Square*, for the Royal Shakespeare Company).

She conducted a series of affairs, mostly short, generally with Frenchmen, nearly always ended decisively by Sonia herself. 'It is with slow steps and immense regret that I part from you,' wrote the distinguished Swiss anthropologist and director of social sciences at Unesco in Paris, Alfred Métraux. He was an old friend of both Bataille and Leiris, who saw him as a wanderer on the face of the earth, courtly, urbane and profoundly melancholy. Métraux and Sonia became lovers at a spring conference in Lisbon, but she realized almost at once that it had been a mistake. 'Will your flowers have thorny stems, or will they be the rare tropical orchids I like so much?' he asked, anticipating the funeral wreath she would compose for him in her last letter. It proved, as he had expected, to be full of flowers, 'not so much tropical as from an English hot-house', vivid and luxuriant as the giver.

PART FOUR

A Game of Masks

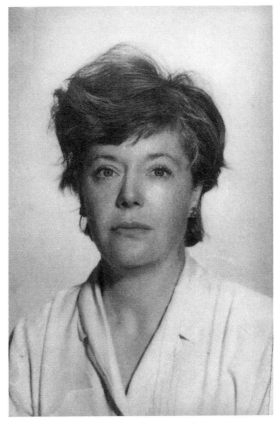

Sonia at the time of her second marriage

On 31 May 1957, the day Sonia strewed farewell flowers for Alfred Métraux, Michel Leiris lay dying in hospital in Paris, having swallowed a massive dose of barbiturates. The three days he spent in a limbo between life and death ended with a recovery that seemed more like a resuscitation. His attempted suicide proved a turning-point, feeding directly into the last two volumes of an autobiographical masterpiece that became a key work for Sonia over the next two decades. 'The whole of *La Règle du jeu* is openly dominated by the consciousness of death,' ran the review in *The Times Literary Supplement*, which she cut out to send to Michel: 'that horror of annihilation that M. Leiris sees as having prevented him from ever committing himself wholeheartedly to life in the body . . . the result has been to lead him to demand from literature satisfactions he would have preferred to meet with in life.'

Sonia embarked on her own final attempt to demand satisfaction from life that summer, which she spent in France visiting friends, including Leiris' colleague Julian Pitt-Rivers. A specialist in bullfights and the tribal rites of Andalusia, Julian divided his time between the University of Chicago, where he was Professor of Anthropology, and a country house which he shared with his Spanish wife near Figeac in the Lot. 'I adore provincial life,' Sonia wrote to Michel from Figeac: 'It's just like a Feydeau farce. Only Julian says I've no gift for field-work.'

Julian Pitt-Rivers in front of his chateau at Figeac

Julian was the younger of two handsome, charming and debonair brothers, both adepts in the cool, teasing, ironic style that is the English equivalent, socially speaking, of a French philosophical position. Julian was the poet and intellectual of the two, Michael (who was a farmer) the funnier and more down-to-earth. They were great-grandsons of the pioneering nineteenth-century anthropologist, General Augustus Pitt-Rivers. His collections furnished two museums (one housed near Blandford, the other at Oxford) as well as the family manor house at Hinton St Mary in Dorset, where the two boys grew up surrounded by bronzes brought back by their great-grandfather from Benin.

They had been accustomed early to a tempestuous home life. Their father, Captain George Pitt-Rivers, was a prominent local fascist, who turned his tithe barn at Hinton into a centre for xenophobic, racist and anti-semitic activity between the world wars. Their mother, who had married very young, ran away while still in her twenties to go on the stage under the name of Mary Hinton, leaving her two small boys with her husband as hostages. Both inherited something of her looks and presence together with the magnetic force of their father, who could be irresistible (at any rate to women) as well as famously, sometimes almost maniacally belligerent (in particular to his sons). Captain Pitt-Rivers was imprisoned as a fascist like Oswald Mosley in 1940, and forbidden to return to Dorset in wartime.

Julian escaped to construct a career abroad. Michael left Oxford to join the Welsh Guards, retiring from the army in 1953 with a distinguished war record and the rank of major to take over a sizeable portion of the vast family estates in Dorset and Wiltshire. He devoted the rest of his life to managing his farmland and ancient woods, planting three million trees and becoming a passionate pioneer conservationist. Both the brothers adored their mother, and learned to distance themselves from their father's depredations by reconstructing him as an absurd, outsize operatic villain. 'I picture from your cryptic mention of King John's House that Father has distrained on Mike again, and left him bedless,' Julian wrote to Sonia on 29 June, 1957: 'It's rather lucky I'm so far away isn't it?'

Michael, who lived in an old hunting lodge (named for Richard Lionheart's brother, King John) at Tollard Royal in Dorset, had followed his father through the courts in rather more sensational circumstances in 1954. He was one of three defendants in the last of the great British homosexual trials

Michael Pitt-Rivers on his estate in Dorset

along with his second cousin, Lord Montagu of Beaulieu, and the foreign correspondent of the *Daily Mail*, Peter Wildeblood. The three were convicted of homosexual activity with airmen in the pleasure gardens known as the Larmer Grounds at Tollard Royal. The Montagu scandal marked the culmination of a vicious campaign in the popular press, sparked off by Sir John Gielgud's arrest the year before, and fuelled by a roll-call of leading homosexuals who were regularly denounced as perverts and crooks in the right-wing tabloids.

The affair became a kind of public show-trial, part of the postwar pattern of social upheaval that produced Senator McCarthy's witch-hunts in the US, and the Algerian conflict that brought France once again to the brink of civil war in the late 1950s. It led to the setting up of the Wolfenden Commission, and the reform bill that finally legalized homosexuality between consenting adults in Britain in 1967. Michael Pitt-Rivers served eighteen months in Maidstone gaol, carrying off the whole barbaric episode with unruffled calm and deadpan humour.

He had the innate elegance, the sensitivity and humorous stoicism Sonia had loved in Peter Watson. He appealed at the deepest level to her chivalrous crusading instincts. 'This is to say I'm going to be married,' she wrote in an uncharacteristically open, unguarded letter to Michel Leiris and his wife Zette at the end of May 1958. 'Naturally I'm in a state of such total confusion I don't know if I'm on my head or my heels, but I do know that the chap is everything that is most admirable in the world . . . His name is Michael Pitt-Rivers (of the dynasty, as Michel would say), and I'm wild with joy.'

Julian, who had introduced the couple and presided over their courtship, was delighted. Practically everyone else was aghast. Like many cultivated, independent and attractive women, Sonia had always had strong and loving relationships with homosexual men. Women, who found their professional lives constantly hampered and restricted in the 1950s and 1960s, easily made common cause with a minority whose activities were punishable by law. To enjoy the company of the suave, witty and sophisticated homosexual contingent in the art- and book world or the theatre was natural enough. But to marry a practising homosexual whose name was a national symbol – whether for infamy or heroism – was more problematic.

'We couldn't believe it. Nobody could,' said Natasha Spender. It cut the ground from under people's feet as drastically as Sonia's engagement to Orwell nine years before. Sonia believed she could restore Michael to his rightful position in the county by an act of commitment that would provide him, in practical terms, with a hostess while making a public mock of the bigotry and hypocritical intolerance that had singled him out as a high-profile scapegoat under an obsolete law. It was the kind of defiant gesture – impulsive, quixotic and easily misunderstood – that suited Sonia. Once again she was needed. Once again she was entering into marriage for nobly disinterested motives.

For people who knew her well, there could be no mistaking her radiant happiness. Cyril, who had reacted badly to news of her first marriage, was no less jealous of her second ('you realise all this prinking is for Michael,' he said crossly to Anne Dunn, when Sonia cut off her long blonde hair). Métraux ran across Sonia again in Paris in early summer, and found her transformed. 'You have never been so beautiful, so intelligent, so brilliant – or more precisely so scintillating,' he wrote: 'long may you continue to scintillate for your sake and ours.'

She was married in Kensington Registry Office on 12 August, cheered on from across the Channel by her French friends. A BAS LA FROUSSE [DON'T BE SCARED] ran a fighting telegram from Marguerite Duras. 'I was petrified just before the wedding,' Sonia wrote two days later to the Leirises from Tollard Royal, 'but now I feel quite simply mad with joy, and happier than I would have believed possible.' She looked ravishing in white silk with black trimmings at the wedding party in the Larmer Grounds for which literary London turned out in force.

The plan was for Sonia to divide her time between

London and the country with side trips to Paris for Michael to meet her French friends. They celebrated with a second wedding party, given by Zette Leiris and Rose Masson (wife of the surrealist painter André Masson), in Paris in the New Year. The couple was setting out to explore South-East Asia on a honeymoon voyage planned to last several months. They travelled with the novelist Vita Sackville-West, aboard the SS *Cambodge*, visiting Angkor Watt armed with introductions from Michel to French archaeologists, and ending up with the sombre return visit to Sonia's childhood home in Calcutta that suddenly made the paradisal places they had seen up to then look like childish make-believe.

They reached home in late spring in time to embark on a hectic round of entertaining and house parties. Friends from London, Paris and New York streamed through Tollard Royal. 'What Sonia did at King John's House was extraordinary,' said Vera Russell, no mean hostess herself and an exacting critic of others in the same role (Vera's ex-husband, the art critic John Russell, had been Sonia's witness at her wedding). 'It was absolute bliss,' said the painter John Craxton, 'totally relaxed, good conversation, plenty to drink, delicious food – like one long *Horizon* party lasting all weekend.' There were picnics, excursions, drives through the rolling Dorset countryside to the sea or Stonehenge and Salisbury Cathedral. 'We mulled it over all the way back on the train,' wrote the journalist Dee Wells, after a weekend at Tollard Royal with her husband Freddy Ayer, '. . . and decided that, all of it, we had never had a better time in our whole lives. We *almost* did a quick turn round at Waterloo to catch the next train back to Salisbury.'

The tricky bit for the Pitt-Riverses was bridging the gap

between quintessentially urban intellectuals like the Ayerses or the Massons or Mary McCarthy – who treated Tollard Royal as an idyllic, exotic, largely unreal, imaginative construct – and the Dorset farmers whose whole existence was bound up with their land. For Sonia, as an outsider, country life never quite lost its farcical side. She didn't know how to talk to the workmen on the estate, who were baffled by her. So were the local gentry. To Michael's neighbours, his wife's cosmopolitan circle seemed as out of place in a rural setting as her Giacometti sculpture (a wedding present from Anne Dunn) in the drawing room at King John's House.

Sonia's brother, Michael Dixon, moved down from London to run the psychiatry department of a large West Country hospital at the start of the 1960s, settling with his wife in an old farmhouse in Wiltshire. He got on well with his Pitt-Rivers brother-in-law, being far more at ease among country people than his sister who knew nothing about the estate, the livestock, the land or the way of life that absorbed her husband. 'She wasn't a country girl,' said Craxton: 'She couldn't get the hang of it.' Neither town nor country at her parties could quite take the other seriously. Each side got the feeling of being sent up by the other. Stories went the rounds featuring the new Mrs Pitt-Rivers as a local version of the girl who invariably gets things wrong in the Bateman cartoons. People repeated the one about how she fell into a hopper, screaming with laughter and asking the farm manager who extricated her: 'Does this plough as well?'

Sonia had once been photographed on a farm for a feature in *Vogue* by Lee Miller, who posed her with rake and wheel-

Anthony Powell, an American friend, and Michael Pitt-Rivers with a bust of Spinoza after lunch at the Chantry, the Powells' house in Somerset

barrow, mowing, making and carting hay, looking in her straight skirt and court shoes like a scaled-down 1950s version of Marie Antoinette at Versailles. Now she was play-acting in earnest. Friends noted an edge of desperation in Sonia on her return from the honeymoon voyage. Their four months away had distanced the couple rather than drawn them together. Michael's unfailing courtesy was tinged with disquiet, Sonia's defensiveness hovered close to aggression. She was drinking too much. The nervous panic that had gripped her before the wedding returned.

She seemed jumpy and strained that spring to Anne Dunn, who came to stay at Tollard Royal with her second husband, the painter Rodrigo Moynihan, and their new baby. Rodrigo remembered Sonia from the outbreak of war, when the Euston Road Venus had taken refuge near Bishop's Stortford, sorting out his household in the country and looking after the small son of his disintegrating first marriage. She and Anne had pursued parallel courses in London and Paris, seeing one another on and off through a decade and more of love affairs and marriages. The Moynihans would become an energizing and stabilizing centrifugal force for Sonia, as her new life fell apart under mounting strain.

For the moment painters, philosophers and poets continued to sit down to dinner at King John's House with French surrealists and local landowners. Tension between their hosts was heightened by Captain Pitt-Rivers, who felt himself in danger of being upstaged by his new daughter-in-law. Police had to be called when he turned up with a horse-whip, threatening to disrupt a pageant at Tollard Royal organized by Sonia to raise funds for the churches of Cranborne Chase. 'I am most upset to hear Father is up to his dirty tricks again . . .' wrote Julian, whose steadfast generosity and kindness sustained her in circumstances he understood perhaps better than anybody else could: 'I do not think anyone in Dorset gives any importance to what Father does or says . . . I personally should be much more alarmed by Father's praise than by his abuse.'

Close friends like Julian and the Moynihans were increasingly aware of the other hidden self behind the brilliant, self-confident chateleine of Tollard Royal. This was the Sonia who defended herself, when threatened, by attacking with a ferocity that startled and dismayed other people.

Anne Dunn painted by Rodrigo Moynihan

Alfred Métraux had suffered cruelly from it. He recognized the distress behind her destructive rage when he told Sonia that his feelings for her had nothing to do with the dazzling front she put on in public, or her biting wit, or even the romantic myth that had grown up around her in Paris. 'Sonia, I loved you so passionately because you seemed to me to be what you are –' he wrote: 'wretchedly vulnerable, cruelly alone, exceedingly desperate. My great and deep tenderness was for this human weakness, not for the outer covering that hides it less and less adequately.'

At the end of December 1959 Beatrice Dixon died. The rift between mother and daughter had long since ceased to matter. In the autumn and winter when Beatrice lay dying, Sonia, who needed courage herself, said her mother's indomitable spirit made her proud. 'The loss of a parent is like an acute illness with prolonged after effects, however much one loves or does not love them,' wrote Cyril, always tender to Sonia in trouble: 'Ancient foundations of the personality crumble and fall in.' Sonia's stepfather, Geoff Dixon, had died a few years before. She and her brother spent late-night sessions together in London, drinking and talking, reviewing their past, looking back to their childhood in India and the mystery of Sonia's parentage.

Her unhappiness by this time was plain to see. It was clear to both the Pitt-Riverses that their marriage was unworkable no matter how much they dreaded offering the world, and in particular Michael's father, any fresh pretext for scandal. Time had eroded the mutual affection and tolerance on which they hoped to build a life that had always seemed unrealistic to their friends. The two tore mercilessly at one another. Sonia's savage sniping at her husband made people feel uncomfortable. She herself once described to me her sense of nausea and helpless, claustrophobic panic at a dinner given by Dorset neighbours for a mutual friend, the novelist, Ivy Compton-Burnett. Michael, who was an incomparable raconteur, mesmerized the table with a relentless diatribe on the horrors of marriage for the benefit of his homosexual host, while Ivy carried on calmly eating, steadying Sonia with innocuous requests to pass the potatoes.

'That marriage won't last,' Ivy had said flatly, the first

time Sonia brought Michael to lunch with her in London: 'That young man won't like all this booky talk.' Writing to commiserate after the final break-up, Mary McCarthy pointed out that she had never seen Sonia's second marriage as more than a game of masks that had gone on too long:

> *The point of such games is they're supposed to end ... This didn't. You went on pretending to be the squire's lady, while the squire went on pretending etc. And under this there was a second level of pretence, which was that the first pretence was terribly amusing, paradoxical, quaint etc. And underneath that – well, I don't know what was underneath that.*

But Mary's brisk, no-nonsense approach ignored the extent to which Sonia had once again been ambushed by her own feelings. The Pitt-Riverses' was a *mariage blanc*. For Michael it remained, as it had begun, a strategic alliance. But for Sonia, however rationally she may have started out, passionate admiration developed into passionate desire. She loved Michael, and she longed to bear his child. Their voyage to the East had trapped them in unbearable proximity, compounded by frustration on one side and disillusionment on the other. When she got back to Dorset, Sonia took an overdose of drugs. For two days she lay unconscious in Salisbury hospital, while no one knew if she would live or die. The episode was successfully hushed up, but the game Sonia played that summer was one she knew she had already lost.

She fled Tollard Royal a year later. Her closest friends were appalled by her misery. Julian Pitt-Rivers sent anxious messages of love and support. Marguerite Duras wrote and telegraphed, urging Sonia to leave England, begging her to join a group of old friends in the country, offering to meet her alone in Paris. In the end Sonia took shelter with the Moynihans, who were camping out with two small children in a farmhouse in Provence. She stayed for two months, shopping in local markets, helping to look after the children, learning how to cook, throwing herself into the life of the household between reckless interludes when she seemed intent on drinking herself to death.

She was working up the courage to return to Dorset for a last attempt to patch things up with Michael. It was short-lived. In the spring of 1961, when the sudden death of Maurice Merleau-Ponty brought back sickening memories of the past, she took another overdose. She recovered but, unlike Michel Leiris, she found no renewal of confidence or purpose in her resuscitation. The continuation of her marriage caused her anguish. Its final collapse was a blow as devastating as George's death. 'It was a shock to her in each case, when the end came, to find how deeply she minded,' said Natasha Spender: 'She didn't realize herself how much she loved them.'

At the end of 1961 Georges Bataille died (Sonia failed to place an English obituary because, as she told Leiris, 'the only people who admire his books over here are me and Francis Bacon'). Leiris said he felt as if, after years in the rear, he had moved up in his sixties to the front line, watching his friends fall around him and waiting for his own turn to come at any moment. In April 1963 it was Alfred Métraux who killed himself, taking an overdose alone in his car in a remote Swiss valley. He had found comfort all his life in the myths of others, wrote Leiris, who might have been thinking of Sonia in the tribute he paid his dead companion:

> *he and his old friend Bataille were among the few who taught me that nothing matters as much as that combination which only a handful of individuals manage to bring off: a fierce love of life joined to a pitiless consciousness of just how derisory that is . . . He was a wanderer, a man who understood most things but took no pride in it, someone who retained in the depths of his being a grief needing consolation . . .*

Sonia returned to her bachelor flat in Percy Street to rebuild her life. She cherished her friends. Over the next decade and more she acquired a tribe of godchildren, including Matthew Connolly, the child of Cyril's remarriage in 1959 to Deirdre Craig ('I first met her at the door of our farmhouse in Sussex,' wrote Deirdre, 'and she was laughing, and wore a bright pink coat. She said: "I'm Sonia." We were instantaneous friends'). Sonia made each of her godchildren feel as if he or she basked in the light of her undivided love and attention. 'She was almost a second mother to me,' said Tom Gross, son of a couple of future literary high-flyers, John and Miriam Gross: 'I was always thrilled to see her. She never ever forgot an occasion, she wrote, she came, she sent letters and presents when I was ill. Sonia was my *only* godparent, but my sister had to have three to make up for my one.'

In the summer of 1962 Sonia organized a prodigiously successful international writers' conference at the Edinburgh Festival, recruiting Malcolm Muggeridge as chairman, with a guest-list headed by Norman Mailer, Rebecca West and Mary McCarthy ('Your performance was simply extraordinary,' Mary wrote afterwards to Sonia: 'Only a person of tremendous good character and sensitiveness could have done half what you did. I think you must have more stability than you know – a bedrock of firmness and decision').

Mary tried to lure her across the Atlantic the year after to work on the *New York Review of Books* ('they badly need a talent like yours, Sonia'). But the Moynihans had already asked her to co-edit another new review, *Art and Literature*, set up largely for Sonia as a modern, international, Paris-based successor to *Horizon*. She found a small, bright, friendly flat in 1963 on the rue des Saints Pères ('it was Percy Street in Paris,' said James Lord), and set about organizing printers, designers and distributors. Rodrigo drew her, Mary McCarthy introduced her to the delights of Parisian dress shows, Marguerite Duras enticed her back into the fevered atmosphere of French intellectual rivalry and exploration.

Her social life spiralled out from Marguerite's literary friends, the American expatriates revolving round Mary and her husband Jim West, and the world of the Leirises' gallery (Zette had taken over the painting stable built up round Picasso by Daniel Kahnweiler, who was her stepfather). Contributors to the new review broadly reflected this mix. Its heterogeneous English element ranged from David Jones to J. R. Ackerley and Jean Rhys, whose novel *Wide Sargasso Sea* (one of the more spectacular literary hits of the decade) Sonia first published in extract in *Art and Literature* in 1964. But she and her fellow editors – Anne Dunn, Rodrigo Moynihan and the American poet John Ashbery – were too diverse to work as a team with the flair, timing and firework brilliance of the triumvirate running *Horizon*. After the first

*Robert Lowell, Sonia, Mary McCarthy and Stephen Spender
(all standing) at a French picnic in 1963*

eighteen months Sonia, who was the kingpin (or queen bee), found she could no longer combine working full-time in Paris with the literary management of the Orwell estate, which took up increasing amounts of attention.

She had set up an Orwell Archive in 1960 as part of the library of University College in London, donating to it all the letters, papers, notebooks and manuscripts she had inherited from George. She had also agreed with some trepidation to edit a collection of Orwell's unpublished writings at the suggestion of his New York publisher, William Jovanovich of Harcourt Brace. Professional assistance came from Ian Angus, the young librarian in charge of the archive, who agreed to help track down Orwell's journalism and letters.

The project expanded from tentative beginnings so rapidly that, by 1965, the mass of material involved required the collaboration of both editors in London.

As a settlement in the divorce finalized that year, Michael Pitt-Rivers bought Sonia a modest two-storey house, number 153 Gloucester Road in South Kensington. She moved back from Paris that summer, bringing as a house-warming present from the Leirises a copy, dedicated to her by the artist, of Picasso's *Les Dames de Mougins*. The plain, solid little house suited her so well it came over the next ten years and more to seem almost an extension of her personality. It had two bedrooms upstairs, and a small basement kitchen (Sonia became an excellent cook) next door to the dining room, which was just big enough for a circular table that held six or eight friends.

But the core of the house was the long drawing room on the ground floor, where Sonia hung the paintings given her over the years by Freud and Bacon (of all the many portraits she sat for, she had kept only one tiny oil sketch by Claude Rogers, which she gave away to the first guest who admired it). It had a polished parquet floor, tall windows and low, white-painted bookshelves, always dotted with vases of fresh flowers. The effect was comfortable, warm and welcoming. It was here that Sonia created over the next decade what Stephen Spender said was the closest thing London possessed to a literary salon, mixing old friends – the Connollys and Spenders, Auden, Edmund Wilson, Robert Lowell, Iris Murdoch, on one memorable occasion two highly competitive Nobel laureates, Saul Bellow and Elias Canetti – with unknown young hopefuls who had often not yet published a first book.

David Plante, who was twenty-five and newly arrived from the US when Sonia first met him, said she welcomed him into the community of writers as if it were a family ('she made me feel that I belonged in London . . . On these evenings, I would leave imagining that I was a promising nephew in her large family'). He was one of a growing band of younger friends – J. G. Farrell, Maya Angelou, the Grosses, Dan and Margaret Jacobsen, David and Rosemary Cairns, my husband and me – who became honorary relations to be criticized and cosseted, familiar figures in the drawing room which, as Plante said, was bright and orderly like Sonia herself. Her dark, disorderly side found its own level in the life she built to balance and contain it in this settled base. 'Before that she was always on the move,' said Anne Moynihan: 'It was the first time she had a house – it was the *only* house she ever had – and she felt more rooted.'

The new house stood within a few minutes' walk of her mother's old headquarters on Tregunter Road and Ivy Compton-Burnett's flat in Cornwall Gardens, equidistant from both, with Francis Bacon's mews studio tucked in behind. The situation could hardly have been better chosen. Francis and Ivy represented the two poles of Sonia's world. Both were old friends of hers. Sonia had once invited the pair to lunch together in Percy Street in the 1950s when Francis was at his racketiest and most disreputable, Ivy stern and forbidding, dressed in voluminous, floor-length black skirts with a military tricorne hat, hair done up in a grey helmet, and the rolled black umbrella that she wielded like a general's baton. Resuming London life in the mid-sixties, Sonia set store by their nearness.

She fell into a pattern of heavy late-night drinking bouts

Ivy Compton-Burnett in her flat

with Francis, and regular afternoon sessions over Ivy's tea-table in the dark flat that always made Sonia feel 'Oh, help!' as soon as the maid opened the door. Ivy's high, bare, grey, practically unheated rooms were as comfortless as Francis's paint-spattered studio with its midden of discarded wrappers, cartons, old newspapers, torn-up photos and empty paint tins. Both lived, literally and metaphorically speaking, by the harsh light of unshaded lightbulbs. Sonia found consolation, more perhaps than ever before in these years, in their bleak, stoical realism.

Francis's philosophy, like his paintings, came with a flourish. 'I have never had any love in the whole of my life,' he said grandly, 'and what's more I don't want any. All I do is cast my rod into the sewers of despair and see what I come up with this time.' Ivy followed much the same programme. Sonia told me Ivy talked about sexual passion with a thoroughness and intimacy that left her – as the younger and ostensibly more experienced of the two – deeply shaken. Her marriage to Michael was never explicitly discussed but Sonia felt there was nothing that Ivy, then over eighty, did not know or understand. Visits to Cornwall Gardens could be as unnerving as the characters in Ivy's books who articulate with lapidary frankness what, in their creator's presence, went without saying:

> '*It is the future we must look to,' said Constance. 'It is useless to pursue the past.'*
>
> '*It is needless,' said Audrey. 'It will pursue us.'*

Francis Bacon in his studio

Sonia introduced selected Parisian friends to her two neighbours. She annoyed Marguerite by taking another of Ivy's admirers, her sole true disciple, the doyenne of the French *nouveau roman*, Nathalie Sarraute, to Cornwall Gardens, where the hostess enchanted her guest by drawing her into the polite world of a mythical Victorian tea party, pouring tea from a silver pot, serving hot, buttered tea-cakes, and declining to talk about anything but rising prices ('maybe all this was just one of my delightful dreams about England?' Mme Sarraute wrote to me, explaining that the whole magical episode made her feel like Alice in Wonderland after she fell down the rabbit hole).

Francis responded more straightforwardly to Michel Leiris, when Sonia first brought them together in Paris. Each recognized something of himself in the other. Francis began a long dialogue in words and on canvas by asking Michel to write a catalogue preface for his show at the Hanover Gallery in 1966. 'Did I tell you we're all reading *L'Age d'homme?*', wrote Sonia, passing on Bacon's request (she subsequently translated Leiris' essay): 'It's agreed to be *the* book of our period by Francis and Lucian, who can talk of nothing else! Funny how painters read with such passion, when they're not in the habit of reading.'

To the end of her life, Sonia, Michel and Francis met regularly to sit talking over companionable lunches in Paris, or on the Leirises' visits to 153 Gloucester Road and the painting studio behind it. They laid plans to visit Scotland and Cornwall together. When Francis found himself invariably prevented at the last minute from joining these Celtic tours, Michel and Zette stopped off instead to see him each time in London. Leiris was the first writer of any

Francis Bacon with Sonia on the Thames at Limehouse

stature to attempt to confront Bacon's paintings, and he returned to them again and again.

'Bacon is a realist *à la* Kafka, *à la* Beckett. Like them, without rhetorical inflation or mythological complication, Bacon expresses the human condition,' he wrote: '. . . a wild passion for life, and the determination to refuse himself nothing, co-exist in him with a lucidity that strips him of all hope.' This tension – between the appetite for life, and the conviction that life is senseless – was central to Leiris' writing. Francis painted it in his portraits of Michel, whose texts he also read and re-read. 'Michel Leiris has shown better than anyone how closely human greatness is linked to mortality,' wrote the painter in a rare, published tribute: 'His work is a personal testament that moves me deeply.'

Michel Leiris by Francis Bacon

Mortality became an all too familiar companion in these years when Sonia faithfully visited old friends, bringing flowers, literary gossip and the capacious, battered old hand-bag crammed with little parcels – new books, useful gadgets, black chocolate, tins of rose cachous or Harrogate toffee – that she unpacked on arrival, like Julia in Orwell's *Nineteen Eighty-Four*. 'I can't thank you enough for your wonderful, life-enhancing visit on Saturday,' wrote her old friend, the writer Francis Wyndham, whose mother was ill and frail: 'Violet *adored* it, and the food (all eaten now!) was un-believably delicious . . . It was like a glamorous and luxuri-ous version of the end of the siege of Mafeking!'

Sonia stayed by Ivy's side to the end (Ivy died at home in her flat in August 1969). She did the same for W. H.

Auden, for Jean Rhys whose last years she transformed, and for Jo Ackerley, embarking in his final decade on the strange, subtle late-flowering that produced *My Father and Myself.* 'Bless your sweet heart, how kind you are and I am sorry you are not happier,' Ackerley wrote in 1965, thanking for a Christmas crate of bottles, and passing on in return a tip he had once had from E. M. Forster:

> But I know nothing about happiness, though I get pleasure from time to time and you, dear Sonia, contribute to that. Many years ago, some forty years ago Morgan Forster, trying to guide me through some miserable love affair, wrote to me 'But happiness may not be your deepest need.' . . . He himself is a happy man, he has cultivated his garden. For many of us, at any rate for me, that has not been possible, but why? It is an unanswerable question . . . I have never been happy, I believe, nor ever can be, I was not equipped to be that, though what my 'deepest need' was and is I do not know. These are things I never say, but I can say them to you, who understand so well . . . were it not for one's friends, life would be past bearing indeed.

PART FIVE

The Widow Orwell

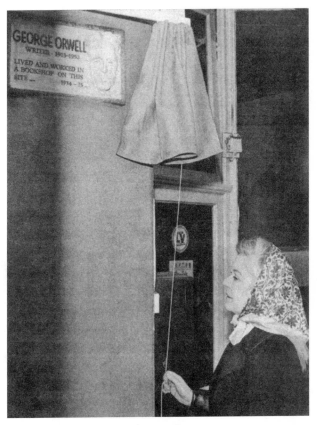

Sonia unveiling a plaque in 1969

Work, like friends, supplied a lifeline. Sonia, who had been preparing herself methodically throughout her period in Paris, plunged immediately on her return to London into the immense labour of tracking down, sorting, sourcing, dating, annotating and structuring the four volumes of Orwell's *Collected Essays, Journalism and Letters*. 'By 1965 she had read – and in a highly intelligent way – every word Orwell ever published,' said Ian Angus: 'We divided the work fifty/fifty.' They split the royalties on the same principle to suit Sonia, who overruled Ian's proposal that he should take only 25 per cent. Like many others, he found her belligerence intimidating until she confronted him head on, demanding to be treated as a human being, and backing her claim by insisting that all editors were equal. 'When Harcourt Brace said they wanted Sonia's name alone on the title page because it would promote sales better, she firmly said no,' Ian wrote, 'and insisted my name was there too.'

Sonia had thought deeply about the format and purpose of a task whose enormity sometimes appalled her. 'But you must do it,' Ivy said with untypical directness when Sonia voiced her misgivings: 'It's your plain duty.' Pangs of anxiety, spells of discouragement and inertia alternated with short-lived spurts of confidence. 'Things are going a bit better now,' she wrote to Leiris in September 1966: 'I get the impression of a pile of dressed stone more or less cut to size rather than a shapeless mass of rocks!'

What worried her was not the drudgery involved but the underlying structural problems and, worse still, the dubious morality of undertaking in the first place to retrieve unpublished or unrevised scraps and pieces which George himself had dismissed as trivial, substandard and over-hasty. 'If people only knew what it cost her,' said Ian, who as the junior partner with no previous editorial experience was amazed by Sonia's professionalism, and the extent of her personal involvement. Officially the ultimate responsibility was hers as Orwell's literary executor, but all editorial decisions were taken jointly.

Together they ruled out the kind of academic approach that seemed premature for a writer whose influence was still so vigorously alive. Together they hit on the chronological arrangement whereby – 'rather unorthodoxly', as Sonia said – letters alternated as they were written with essays and articles. These were major steps into as yet uncharted territory. Both were painfully aware that the shape they chose to give to this collection of frequently obscure, forgotten, sometimes wholly unknown writings would crucially affect Orwell's future power and reputation. Ian remembered agonizing, seemingly endless deliberations conducted by telephone, or sitting side by side confronting a sea of papers on Sonia's dining table:

Every single item we discussed together, and some items we discussed for weeks on end until we finally agreed. Sonia's actual words were: 'I want it to read like a novel, so people won't put it down.' It wasn't smoothness she wanted, it was that nothing

Ian Angus, Orwell's archivist and co-editor of his Collected Essays,
*who kept the record straight for Sonia, too, collecting papers,
answering queries, correcting misinformation and mistakes for twenty
years after her death*

*should be included that the reader might find boring and stop
reading. I suspected that was how Cyril thought each number of
Horizon should be. At the same time she was terrified it might
pull George down instead of building him up. She was determined
to do nothing that could undermine him.*

In the event she need not have worried. The two editors
were widely congratulated on an impeccable performance
('it is a model of unobtrusive learning, of editorial tact,'
wrote George Steiner in the *New Yorker*: 'The general index
alone is worth the price of the set'). Reviewers agreed that
Orwell had been revealed, both as a man and a writer, more
clearly than ever before. 'He stands alone in every sense,'
wrote Malcolm Muggeridge, voicing the general view that
the new edition shifted the balance away from its subject's
uneven fictional achievement towards his uncanny ability
as essayist and journalist to gauge the temperature of his
time. Over the next decade it did more than anything since
Orwell's death to establish him as one of the most influential
writers of the twentieth century. 'When, in 1968, the four
volume collection of his *Essays, Journalism and Letters* was
published . . .' wrote Peter Lewis, speaking for a whole
generation of readers who grew up on the paperbacks, 'it
was recognized that in Orwell's hands journalism was raised
to the level of literature.'

Sonia's anxiety had been unspeakable. Ian said that the
period immediately before publication was the worst three
or four months of his life. Sonia, strung-up and exhausted,
fearful that they had irretrievably damaged her husband's
reputation, turned to him for a reassurance he could not
give. 'She was terrified, frightened to death, that it would

be greeted with scorn,' said Ian: 'She was beside herself. It was appalling to watch.' More than the usual quota of misunderstandings, botch-ups and cross-purposes at the publishers added to the general tension. Ian, who had come closer than anyone else to understanding the complexity of her response during three years' hard labour, now bore the brunt of her dismay ('curiously enough Sonia's drinking at this point did not increase, though she was frequently in a state of near-hysteria'). On the day of publication, her relief at the books' reception was as overwhelming as her previous apprehension. She took Ian and three friends out to dinner, and ended up blind drunk.

From now on, Sonia came under increasing pressure. The *Collected Essays* produced more than a dozen critical works, and renewed demand for the biography Orwell had expressly forbidden in his will. Sonia tentatively approached Richard Ellmann, who was initially enthusiastic in the wake of his *James Joyce* but eventually changed his mind in favour of Oscar Wilde. The Orwell Archive had been set up for the benefit of scholars prepared to give an assurance that they had no biographical intentions. When Peter Stansky and William Abrams (who had consulted the archive in the course of research for a book on English writers in the Spanish Civil War) ignored this undertaking, Sonia and the trustees withdrew access and withheld permission to quote.

Stansky and Abrams felt, like all biographers, that knowledge should be free, and that their right of access overrode all other considerations. But Sonia knew at first hand how fiercely her husband had guarded his own and his family's privacy. She told Ian that George had been so infuriated by a life of Joseph Conrad written by his widow that he hurled it across the room, saying to Sonia (who was mystified): *'Never do that to me.'*

'I am very proud of having been George's wife, and in general feel very guilty about him, which I believe is usual for widows,' Sonia wrote to Ian, explaining why it mattered so much to her to keep faith with Orwell. She had not been consulted about the anti-biographer clause in his will, which caused her great and growing misery to the day she died. In 1972, when Stansky and Abrams published the first volume of their life of Orwell, Sonia felt they left her no option save to appoint an official biographer. Her choice of the political economist Bernard Crick was an impulsive decision which, like many of her defiant gestures, she later came to regret.

Orwell had loved her for her passionate, instinctive responses. But he had also had confidence in her good sense, and in the meticulous thoroughness that deeply impressed the two people who worked most closely with her, Ian Angus and Mark Hamilton, Orwell's literary agent at A. M. Heath. 'No detail was too small for her attention,' said Hamilton who, like Ian, acquired considerable respect for Sonia's professional acumen in the course of working with her for more than fifteen years: 'She gave a great deal of time to running George's affairs. She wasn't difficult, she was very businesslike. She had been a bloody good editor at Weidenfeld, and she knew a lot more than most authors. She read *everything*.'

She vetted all proposals, checked contracts, oversaw anthology sales, scrutinized translations, scripts and selections herself. When the *Collected Essays* were published in 1968, she had turned down a substantial sum from George's old friend, the owner of the *Observer*, David Astor, for fear that serialization might distort or sensationalize the contents (the *Observer* wanted to print Orwell's scathing account of his experiences at prep school, 'Such, such were the Joys'). Her prime concern was always for the totality of Orwell's work. Hamilton said she had refused a major Hollywood deal for *Nineteen Eighty-Four*, and invariably rejected lucrative offers from foreign publishers interested only in that and *Animal Farm*. She wrested French rights from Gallimard, who kept the earlier books technically in print but unavailable ('I hear you wrote an article that made the Gallimards go white with rage,' wrote Marguerite, who had her own problems with the same firm, 'which cheered me up no end').

By this time Sonia knew Orwell's work backwards. In the last year of his life, when the American publishers tried in vain to make him agree to changes in *Nineteen Eighty-Four*, she had witnessed George's horror of having his work 'mucked about' in the interests of making it more accessible. Throughout the 1970s, as Orwell's fame grew, she consistently discouraged speculative publishers, theatrical adaptors, film producers, all the commercial developers anxious to cash in on a hot property in the run-up to 1984. Rejected applicants inevitably found her approach tiresome and highhanded.

Orwell had put her in an impossible position but it was her reputation, not his, that suffered. Her attempts to discourage the kind of exploitation he could never have envisaged in his lifetime landed her in increasing trouble. People retaliated, as they had long ago when they found her taking decisions at *Horizon*, with stories about her bossiness and stridency. Her drinking, which could have been overlooked in a man, was cited as proof of general incapacity in a woman. These years saw the beginning of the myth that, since her death, has re-created the Widow Orwell as a monster of obstinacy, greed and wilful obstruction.

I first met her in 1970. As a young biographer newly commissioned to write my first book, I was learning the trade by interviewing the highly alarming friends of my subject, who was Dame Ivy Compton-Burnett. People warned me to expect a hard time from the notorious Mrs Orwell. When she arrived on the dot of one for lunch, I was taken aback by her unexpectedly demure appearance in what I soon realized was her standard uniform of dark skirt, woolly cardigan and plain, high-necked white blouse. She looked me over, summed up my skimpy Biba frock and platform shoes with a sardonic, wheezy sigh, lifted her shoulders in a Gallic shrug, knocked back her first gin, and launched in her rich, gravelly voice into a vehement denunciation of the law courts.

She had been reading *Bleak House*, which sounded from her description like a ribald Dickensian preview of the jailhouse scenes in Tom Wolfe's *Bonfire of the Vanities*. Being a lawyer's daughter, I was enchanted by her comical and chillingly authentic account of a legal system that left litigants crushed, broken or buried alive under mountains of paper. It was the first of innumerable long, boozy, convivial meals, and we parted at the end of it with enthusiastic mutual assurances that neither of us would under any circumstances ever go to law. I often thought of that first meeting in the next ten years when Sonia's life was increasingly darkened and ultimately destroyed by legal and other battles over Orwell.

At first there was no obvious sign of danger ahead. Sonia was an enchanting friend, tonic and stimulant, encouraging, attentive, infinitely resourceful in a crisis. My chief memory from those first years is of the fun we had at her place or ours, or when she stayed with us two summers running in a borrowed cottage in the country. She had the knack of turning the simplest occasion – a scratch lunch, a walk, a blackberrying expedition – into a celebration. In the summer of 1973 she visited us on campus at the University of East Anglia, where my husband John had a writing fellowship. We were poor authors with no regular income or jobs, living on our wits with a baby in two rented rooms in London. Sonia arranged a dinner invitation from the university's most distinguished visiting professor, Angus Wilson, who lived sixty miles away on the far side of Suffolk.

We crammed into her little car with the baby and set out across the hot, dry, biscuit-coloured East Anglian plain. We had started late. After a while we seemed to be lost as well. Nervous tension rose in the car when suddenly a balloon appeared, motionless in what had by now become a pale, still, midsummer twilight: a tiny striped balloon with a basket beneath, suspended far away against one of those vast skies that always fill three-quarters of the horizon in that flat landscape. It was the first hot-air balloon I had ever seen outside a picture book. It seemed quite unreal, coming from nowhere, as if by magic. This was the title of our host's new novel, and we felt he had himself somehow conjured it up or sent it as a signal that we were on the right road at last.

He turned out to live in the middle of a wood in an ancient woodcutter's cottage with an uneven floor and windows so low you almost had to kneel to look out of them. We sat in the garden, drinking champagne, among tumbling, sweet-scented old roses that breasted up against the hedge on one side and spilled out into the wood on the other, when suddenly the balloon materialized again, hanging low over the cottage. 'We had never seen one there before,' Angus wrote, describing that magical evening when he and Sonia rediscovered all their old fondness for one another, 'and we have never seen one since. But I could tell from her expression that the whole incident had taken her in delight away from the tensions that so preyed upon her.'

All her friends realized that Sonia was driven by demons she could not fully control. Fear, suspicion and hostility lay increasingly close to the surface. Insecurity or drink released an aggression that made her many enemies. But beneath the trappings of the hardened old warhorse you could still see traces of the impetuous young thoroughbred, who had enchanted Leiris and others a quarter of a century before. 'I glimpsed a Sonia . . . with a vitality, even a beauty that is wholly new . . . a fiery impassioned woman leading men into battle!' wrote a French friend, picturing Sonia in romantic mode as a ferocious modern Marianne or Joan of Arc: 'We need women like you, who activate our energies and lead us into combat, sorceresses and dynamiters!'

Sorceress or not, Sonia's dynamite tended to ignite at random in private, or at parties in angry tirades often directed at a particular victim, generally male, whom she singled out for attack. 'It was like having a friend who kept a wild animal as a pet, and let it off the leash from time to time,' said Miriam Gross (who, like Deirdre Connolly, grew very close to Sonia in these last years). Sonia's nephew compared her impact, when she turned on him for no reason he could understand, to a drive-by shooting. David Plante, who wrote a book about how it felt to be one of her victims, analysed what lay behind her venom in a second, unpublished memoir:

> But, if Sonia was hard on others, she was harder on herself. How she endured, day after day, her awareness of her own failings, I can't imagine . . . I believe she lived in a state of constant and searing self-consciousness. It was this self-consciousness that made her so hard on herself, and that underlined her need to be so deliberately and shockingly honest. The Sonia I knew was, at her own expense, as incapable of dishonesty as she was incapable of escaping that severe self-consciousness . . . her honesty was at her own expense because it was never forgiving of her own failings, was a kind of punishment for them.

It meant she both understood and forgave the failings of others. If she was profoundly fatalistic about her own disasters, Sonia confronted other people's with energy and determination. Her house was still the first port of call for friends in the throes of a marriage break-up, work crisis or writer's block, the loss of a parent or partner. When Francis Bacon's lover, George Dyer, killed himself in Paris on the occasion of the great Bacon retrospective at the Grand Palais in 1971, Sonia saw Francis through it with Michel Leiris ('we had some strange moments, didn't we, but oddly enough it was almost bearable because of you,' she wrote a few days later, describing the funeral for Michel). Francis painted George afterwards, writhing and vomiting in the bathroom of their hotel on the rue des Saints Pères. Sonia spent evenings with him in London, drinking and going over what had happened. 'We talked about George and guilt for a very long time,' she wrote to Leiris, without specifying which George, or whose guilt.

Her response to suffering or sickness could not have been more delicate. Her letter to me, on my father's sudden, violent death, came from someone who had never blunted or blurred her own sensitivity to shock and horror. 'One had the feeling you'd somehow managed to be there, with one,' David Sylvester wrote, when his father died: 'It was truly generous.' Sonia's generosity was always primarily imaginative. 'She was masterful –' said Ian Angus, 'masterful is the word – at eliciting what was wrong, and doing something practical about it.' 'Now what can I say,' wrote the writer Jessica Mitford, after one of those extraordinary visitations from Sonia that lifted her friends' spirits like the sun coming out: 'only, Sonia, that you are probably the kindest and most generous person I've ever met, mostly because you seize on, or rather grasp what one really longs for . . . and then dash forward and put them into action. The things one longs for, I mean.'

These things were often intangible, but Sonia had almost a genius for localizing wants and needs people didn't even know they had. She understood the consoling power of silliness and frivolity. '*Of course she bought champagne!*', she said indignantly, when someone complained about a hard-up friend squandering a much-needed cheque. I remember quantities of absurd little presents, odds and ends of pretty flowered china, delicious things to eat and drink, books above all. She would arrive with the latest hardbacks we wouldn't have thought of buying (and couldn't have afforded in any case), her bag bulging with toys for our daughter Amy (who was her thirteenth and last godchild), and tiny sample bottles of French perfume for me. She gave me a plastic spindryer for salad as soon as they appeared in the shops, and a double-spouted sauceboat from a French supermarket which I still use. 'I can't look anywhere in this house without seeing something Sonia bought me,' said Violet Powell, 'to make up for the loss of a teapot she had seen me smash.'

Sonia with Lady Violet Powell,
photographed by Anthony Powell,
at the Chantry

None of these things cost much of anything but time, effort and affection. People assumed Sonia was a wealthy woman in those days, but she never lived like one. Wine flowed freely at her parties, or when she entertained friends to meals she shopped for, cooked and served herself in her cramped basement dining room. Otherwise she spent next to nothing on herself. She came back from France once with a chic little Paris frock for Amy, but I never saw her wear anything like that herself. 'Sometimes her clothes are worn and darned in patches,' David Plante noted in the 1970s: 'She has one winter overcoat.' The only regular holidays I remember her taking were the motoring trips with the Leirises throughout the late 1960s and 1970s, when Sonia acted as chauffeur, putting up at modest hotels and touring Celtic sites in Ireland, Scotland, Wales, Cornwall and Brittany. When she travelled abroad, she nearly always stayed with old friends, the Leirises or Marguerite in Paris, Jessica Mitford or Mary McCarthy (until the two quarrelled over Mary's hostile review of Orwell's *Collected Essays*) in the US.

In the ten years I knew Sonia, her sole extravagance was Jean Rhys. Sonia had given Jean confidence as a writer by publishing in the first issue of *Art and Literature* part of the first draft of *Wide Sargasso Sea*. The novel would bring its author immediate and lasting fame when it was finally published two years later. Before that, Jean had lived for years in poverty and isolation in a Devon village called Cheriton Fitzpaine, forgotten or assumed to be dead by the literary world. Sonia wrote to offer help when the novel came out in 1966. Jean, who was seventy-six years old, asked for a holiday, and Sonia gave her one. 'She arranged everything, like a fairy godmother,' wrote Jean's biographer,

Carole Angier. 'Sonia Orwell made more difference to her life than anyone else,' wrote Jean's publisher, Diana Athill:

She didn't just pay hotel bills: she did all the tipping in advance. She explained to the management the special kinds of attention this old lady would need, she booked hairdressers and manicurists, she bought pretty dressing-gowns, she saw to it that the fridge was full of white wine and of milk for Jean's nightcap, she supplied books, she organized visitors . . . From time to time she even did the thing she most hated . . . took Jean shopping for clothes . . . It was thanks to her that I got a glimpse of how enchanting Jean must have been as a young woman (when happy).

Sonia saw to it that Jean took her place for the first time among her professional peers. 'What an absolute darling she is!' Iris Murdoch wrote after a lunch Sonia gave for the two of them. Jean took to her new life like a parched flower in water, shedding her wary, defensive mannerisms, opening and expanding with pleasure and assurance. 'I thought her changed out of recognition – *so* communicative and happy and at ease. It was really wonderful . . .' Francis wrote to Sonia. 'She had loved her day's shopping, and talked about writing another book. I can't tell you how marvellous I think it is of you to have organized this holiday for her. Nobody else could have done it – you were really inspired.'

For the rest of Jean's life Sonia organized annual winter holidays in London, laying on a round of shopping and parties, and keeping up a steady flow throughout the rest of the year of letters, visits and parcels ('chocolate eggs at Easter, partridges and *marrons glacés* at Christmas, a flood of presents whenever she came to Cheriton Fitzpaine'). She brought with her a whiff of Paris, the city where Jean had been happiest. The two would come back from champagne lunches together, gossipy and giggly, full of silly jokes and stories. 'I

Jean Rhys

felt sad that you'd never known her as early as I did,' Sonia wrote after Jean's death to David Plante, 'because there's no describing her charm, at moments, in those days, and also no describing how selfless she could be when she thought about her friends or other people or, indeed, people in general.'

Sonia had the power to make Jean young again. Where other people made her feel despised or threatened, Sonia gave support, admiration, unconditional approval. 'Jean could come out of hiding with her,' wrote Angier. 'She trusted Sonia with more of herself – her memories, her real feelings – than she had ever trusted anyone . . .' Jean could be spiteful and fractious, like a child, but Sonia gave no hint of impatience or boredom. She didn't want thanks, or even acknowledgement. The spectacle of Jean's happiness was enough for her. It had a kind of magical, healing power, as if wounds and hurts Sonia never spoke of were somehow assuaged by seeing Jean revive again in spite of a traumatic past.

'It was just part of the colonial pattern,' Sonia explained, when I asked why Jean's parents in the West Indies had shipped her back to England, then apparently abandoned her to struggle alone as a teenager. 'White children had to be sent home to be educated . . . Her parents begged her to come back to Dominica . . . but Jean . . . wouldn't go back, and thought she could manage and fend for herself.' For Sonia, Jean's break with her family, her courage and loneliness, her lack of support and mistrust of other people were familiar ground. In some sense she saw herself reflected in Jean's distorting mirror.

As Jean grew older, frailer and more exacting, Sonia redoubled her attentions. She drew up rosters of friends to lunch with her, and drop in for drinks in the evening. She laid on people to take her shopping, read to her, respond to her slightest whim. I was detailed to collect her washing. David Plante, roped in to help her clarify and organize material that would form the nucleus of her new book, wrote a harrowing account of Jean drinking and raving, growing steadily more muddled, maudlin and aggressive, lashing out in desperation and frantic self-doubt.

'Sonia knew Jean's worst witch-like moods very well,' wrote Angier. When Jean tested her friends' indulgence to the limit and beyond, Sonia remained calm and detached, coordinating the support campaign from a distance, analysing tactics ('this is the way a lonely person behaves when she finds herself at last in company'), rallying the helpers with encouragement and sound advice ('you must, must, must protect yourself now,' she wrote to Diana Melly when Jean turned savage, as she almost always did in the end to anyone who tried to help her). If Sonia recognized her own worst fears in Jean, the recognition made her infinitely compassionate. She did everything in her power, from the day they met until Jean died in 1979, to make her life come right.

It was Sonia's own life that, for reasons nobody could understand, went horribly wrong. In the spring of 1977, she put her house on the market, stored her furniture and books, and left England without warning for Paris. She rented a single damp furnished room, on the ground floor of a block on the rue d'Assas, with a basement kitchen that smelt of escaping gas. She had no oven and no bath. People who visited her there were bewildered. Parisian gossip said that the wealthy Widow Orwell was playing at being poor, on a whim, from an inverted sense of chic. Sonia herself gave no explanation beyond implying that she had sold up for tax reasons, mentioning accountants and lawyers, and hinting at complications too frightful to grasp.

Sonia's accountant was still Jack Harrison, the man George had engaged shortly before he died to sort out his tax problems. Over the next three decades Harrison remained her business manager. He was genial, expansive, reassuring, the essential third man with Mark Hamilton and Ian Angus in the team Sonia put together to run Orwell's rapidly expanding estate. She relied on their efficiency as advisers, and she liked them as people. She warmed to Mark for his wry wit, his deceptively mild, unassuming manner, and the solid rock underneath. Sonia spent holidays with the Hamiltons, and commissioned their young son to make a doll's house as a parting present for my small daughter ('so Amy won't forget me in a hurry,' she wrote, as if she didn't expect to return). She loved Ian for his intellectual acuteness, elegance and sensitivity, and for his underlying gentleness. After a sticky start, when he treated her as a ferocious, man-eating dragon, the two became fast friends and confidants.

Jack Harrison invited her to family dinners on Friday nights in Golders Green. 'He was very kind to me, and I came to look on him as a friend as well as an accountant,' Sonia wrote later. Their relationship went back to the days immediately after George's death when Sonia, knocked off balance by shock and grief, had needed someone to turn to. Its origins lay even further back in childhood pain and longing. 'I did see him as a sort of father-figure,' she wrote in October 1978, explaining that her father and stepfather – a freight-broker and an accountant respectively – had never been there to look after her: 'I was delighted when Jack Harrison assumed this role.'

Her confidence in him, as always with someone she trusted, was unbounded. He was the only financial advisor she ever had, and in her eyes he was the best. Michael Pitt-Rivers and the Moynihans consulted him on her recommendation. He looked after Jean's financial affairs and handled the appeal fund Sonia raised when Cyril Connolly died, to pay off his debts and provide a capital sum for his widow and children. 'He gave her a great sense of security,' said Anne Moynihan.

Harrison was Jewish, which enhanced his appeal for Sonia whose uncritical commitment to the Jewish people went back to her feelings for Eugene Vinaver. In the 1970s she travelled to Poland, staying in Warsaw and visiting a concentration camp with Marguerite Duras, who was appalled. 'What did you expect?' Sonia asked angrily: 'What? That it wouldn't be quite as horrible as you imagined?' She identified absolutely with the Jews as with all outsiders and rejects. She lived her life on the principle articulated by Eugene's father in his own battles for liberation: 'We Jews are a small people, but we have one powerful weapon – despair.'

Sonia may have rejected the Catholic church, but she retained her capacity for blind faith. According to the lawsuit she brought against Jack Harrison shortly before she died, she was content to be told what to do like a child when it came to money ('We were both of us complete babies about financial matters,' she wrote of herself and George, 'and were only too delighted if someone else looked after them for us'). Although she was the nominal managing director of George Orwell Productions, she claimed to have remained as passive in the running of the company as she was active on the literary side. All royalties were paid directly to the company by the agents. Sonia never even signed a company cheque. 'I left all financial matters in the hands of Jack Harrison, and paid any money I myself earned into the company on their advice.'

Sonia paid maintenance, school and college fees through

George Orwell Productions for George's adopted son, Richard Blair, who lived with his aunt Avril in Scotland. She corresponded with her stepson, sending Christmas and birthday presents, but making no attempt to interfere in his upbringing. Distances were too great for them to meet often during his childhood, and the two never became close. The company bought Richard a house when he left agricultural college to take a job with Massey Ferguson, and continued paying him a small quarterly allowance. 'I must point out, however, that any allowance is entirely voluntary on our part,' Harrison wrote sternly in 1966, observing that the money had been overspent, enclosing an advance of £12.10s and issuing a warning that, in case of further misdemeanour, 'I shall have to reconsider the position.'

The company also contributed to Binning and Dixon finances, making occasional loans, assigning a small allowance to Sonia's mother (who was, after all, Orwell's mother-in-law), and buying the little house in which she spent her last years with three of her siblings. Sonia, riddled by guilt at the idea of spending Orwell's money on her own family, dreaded nerving herself to plead their cause with the prudent Harrison. The modest sums paid over, and Sonia's extreme anxiety about them, inevitably struck her family as grudging and ungenerous. Tensions of this sort were what made Sonia feel so much at home with Ivy Compton-Burnett. 'Well, the English have no family feelings,' says the author's alter ego, Miss Mitford in *Parents and Children*. 'That is, none of the kind you mean. They have them, and one of them is that relations must cause no expense.'

Sonia herself asked Harrison for money reluctantly, and only for exceptional items like a car or a major piece of clothing. According to her subsequent legal claim, she attended the company's brief board meetings when she was in London as a formality, asking no questions, signing any papers put before her, and accepting without cavil the sum proposed as her stipend. Sonia's monthly cheque from George Orwell Productions, which had started off in 1950 at just over £40, had risen by the end of the decade to £150. This included any salary she herself brought in from editing or reviewing. By 1977 the sum stood at £750 a month.

'I was continually assured by Jack Harrison that I must go on working,' Sonia wrote, explaining why she believed the royalties produced by spiralling American paperback sales of *Animal Farm* and *Nineteen Eighty-Four* to be largely illusory: 'I was informed that due to tax this amounted to far less than appeared.' By 1971 the two novels had sold twenty million copies between them in paperback. Sales settled at around a million copies a year in the early part of the decade, increasing again in the run-up to 1984. According to Orwell's English publisher, the combined income brought in by all the foreign authors on Secker & Warburg's list – including among others Kafka, Günter Grass, Heinrich Böll, Thomas Mann, Italo Svevo, Alberto Moravia, Colette and André Gide – 'added up to a sum roughly equal to one half of the earnings of George Orwell'. By the end of the 1970s, the income brought in by the Orwell books amounted to well over £100,000 a year.

Sonia was still the same person who had said, when Bill Coldstream urged her to raise the question of payment at *Horizon* nearly forty years before, that she couldn't bring herself to mention money. She told her lawyer in retrospect that she had sold her house in 1977 because Jack Harrison advised her that tax benefits, after a year's residence abroad, would enable her to buy a flat in central London and another in Paris. When she left the country, he replaced her as managing director at a company board meeting on 1 April 1977. It was only after he crossed the Channel to visit her in December that she realized for the first time that she was no longer even nominally in charge of the company. 'Jack Harrison said he thought, roughly, I was worth about £100,000 and added, "Less a quarter, Sonia. I wouldn't lie to you," with an odd grin.' He explained that, at various points over the past twenty years, she had signed over to him 25 per cent of the shares, together with 60 per cent of the voting rights, in George Orwell Productions.

At the April 1977 board meeting, an urgent resolution was tabled by Jack Harrison for action to be taken to exploit Orwell's copyrights before they ran out. The following summer the board met without Sonia. Mark Hamilton, who represented her, reported back that Harrison had moved to maximize profits on a film deal for *Nineteen Eighty-Four*. 'Jack Harrison suddenly . . . became conscious of the copyright running out,' Sonia wrote (Orwell's copyrights were due to expire in the year 2000), 'and he must have determined to exploit the estate for all it was worth which, in his eyes, would have been through films.'

This kind of proposal was anathema to Sonia. She consulted a solicitor, who advised her to initiate the lawsuit that shadowed her last years. Jack Harrison vigorously defended the proceedings, arguing that all of his actions in running the company had been with the express or implied approval of Sonia, and in accordance with the wishes of George Orwell. Sonia had no capital except the proceeds from the sale of her house (already earmarked for legal expenses), but shortage of funds was the least of her worries. What tormented her was the fact that she had lost control of the company responsible for Orwell's copyrights.

'I now feel I've just been sucked into some gigantic machine which pays no attention to the fact that I am existing and suffering: I don't count any more, nor does George,' she wrote to one of her oldest friends, Diana Witherby, as the wheels of the law began to grind: 'I just feel so disloyal to poor George.' Her health failed at this point, and her unhappiness was horrible to see. Old friends could only look on appalled at the sea of troubles that threatened to engulf her. 'Oh Hilary!' she wrote to me from Paris on 2 April 1979: 'I'm beginning to feel that I'll never, ever get out of the mess I'm in. The LAW . . . I am being crowded out with papers, papers, PAPER.'

She had reached the final stages of her successful suit against the Gallimards, who spread disobliging rumours about her. She was also beginning to worry about Bernard Crick's life of Orwell (now nearing completion), which made it clear that crispness, lucidity and learning in the field of political economy could not guarantee the kind of imaginative and emotional openness essential in a biography. Depression ate up her energy. She said she felt she was in some kind of special open prison for high-class fools.

She spent much time alone, in bed, reading Victor Hugo. Money was tight. Her lawyer told me that Sonia had had to write to Jack Harrison the year before to ask for £150 to buy a warm overcoat. The loss of her house meant that her roots had been pulled up again, as they had been at intervals throughout her childhood and youth. 'My worst moment, in many ways,' she told Diana, 'was waking up one morning and saying to myself, "Today I'm sixty, and I haven't got a home."' When she asked permission to rent the little flat next to hers, so as not to have to receive friends in her bedroom, she was told it would put too great a strain on the company's resources. She missed her friends in England, and poured her feelings into correspondence. 'Her letters were affectionate,' wrote David Plante, 'and as if filled with small fresh bunches of flowers.'

She wrote to me often, entering into my life, somehow turning the complaints and misfortunes of a hard-up writer with three small children, a book on hand and a living to earn, into a riotous, absurd, oddly comforting comic saga. Every now and then she added a brief lament of her own. 'My news is very bad indeed,' she wrote on 17 October 1979:

> *The first time the case can be heard is January 1981! I spent a lot of my youth in a bed-sitter and thought that was somehow alright. But I cannot tell you how I resent spending my last years in one, for they are my last years, I'm sure . . . Since this case started people have been married, divorced, had and been cured of cancer, moved their flats, taken new jobs etc. etc., while I seem to remain in some circle of Limbo where immobility is the punishment.*

Michel and Zette Leiris were a comfort. They asked her regularly to their country house at St Hilaire, where she slept in a white bedroom full of Picassos and spent hours (as she always did on visits to friends) tending the garden. Michel made her laugh ('It was a lovely afternoon and blow me down if for about three hours I was extremely happy

Sonia with David Plante at a party for
Francis Bacon

and clean forgot the Law and all its perils!' she wrote after a visit to him at the Musée de l'Homme). She gave a small seventy-eighth birthday party for him with Francis as guest of honour. Both agreed that *Frêle Bruit* – the final volume of Michel's autobiography, which opens and closes with death – was truly Shakespearian. Sonia said it marked one of the high points of her life.

She drove the Leirises on the last of their Celtic journeys to Brittany in the summer of 1979, when Michel noted in his diary that she was sometimes too exhausted to leave the car. 'For two years now I haven't drawn a breath without such moral pain and I simply don't know what to do,' she wrote to Diana. Jean Rhys had died in May. In August our oldest friend, the novelist J. G. Farrell, was drowned while fishing from rocks off the Irish coast. 'Jim's death certainly makes everything seem sadder,' wrote Sonia, refusing my attempt to find comfort in the happiness of his last months:

> *I mean the unbearable bit of death is that not only will we not see Jim again and that's just terrible, if only for his smile and giggles and sudden dogmatic outbursts and his whole general elegance which did so enhance any room he was in, but also that he won't see anything again and, in a way, he was pleased to be alive I always felt and would have gone on getting his own pleasures out of life.*

She herself said that reading, her prime consolation since childhood, was now her only joy. All through the spring and summer I posted the books submitted for the Booker prize (I was a judge that year) across the Channel as I finished them. Her comments were succinct, acute, full of pith, recalling the bloody good publisher's editor she had once been. 'I think it's far and away his best to date,' she wrote of *A Bend in the River* by her friend V. S. Naipaul: 'His picture of whole communities crawling over the face of the earth is magnificently grand and gloomy like some elegy for the Flood.'

At the beginning of 1980 Sonia came back to England to

spend the final months of her life camping out in hotels, friends' spare bedrooms, and eventually public-hospital wards. She longed for a place of her own again, to unpack her books and pictures, but lawyers and accountants had, as she said, made her a refugee ('like someone in Vidia's book, I don't seem to be legal anywhere'). She had always loved Homer's Odysseus for his resilience, his resourcefulness, his rootless, restless exile's sensibility, and his dignity in defeat. She said he was her favourite character in fiction, quoting him often: 'Bear up my heart, for you have known worse than this.'

She made her base in our flat, seeing almost no one except doctors and lawyers. She was staying with us when the doctors told her she had cancer. She sat down, like Julia defying her own grim fate in *Nineteen Eighty-Four*, to paint her face. Putting on fresh make-up was, metaphorically speaking, always Sonia's first move in time of trouble. She said she wouldn't mind dying but – lifting her shoulders in the familiar cynical French shrug – she had no intention of doing so until she had seen Crick's biography published and the lawsuit settled.

She was suing Jack Harrison and George Orwell Productions for substantial sums of money and also, in a separate lawsuit, for the ownership of Orwell's copyrights. Harrison claimed that it had been agreed with Orwell that GOP should own and exploit the copyrights, and that Orwell had offered him 25 per cent of the shares in the company. There had been no witness to this conversation, and no time to draw up a deed, because Orwell died the next day. The company acted ever afterwards as if it owned the copyrights but no subsequent agreement to that effect was ever signed. Sonia's solicitors were confident of winning her case.

But, as it became less and less likely that Sonia would live to attend the hearing in January 1981 – or be strong enough to stand a gruelling cross-examination in the witness box if she did – they advised her that all she could do was negotiate a settlement on the defendants' terms. Since Sonia's sole priority was to redeem herself in her own eyes by justifying Orwell's faith in her, she agreed. Meanwhile she went over the proofs of the biography, sitting up in bed in a room at the top of our stairs. I carried them up to her in plastic bags. The past seemed to hang over the house like a black cloud. She had a brain tumour, and saw figures I couldn't see in the corners of the room.

Sonia didn't explain her predicament. None of her friends or family understood what was happening. Nor did I at the time, though I knew very well we were watching a tragedy. Anne Moynihan said she got her first glimmering of the truth only when the taxi, in which they were going out to lunch, deposited them at the Royal Marsden cancer hospital. 'How absurd to have this in the waiting-room,' said Sonia, leafing through a copy of *Country Life*, 'when there is no future.' Sonia's brother Michael wrote to make up after some sort of estrangement, suggesting a holiday in France together, describing how he had just had a tooth out and could feel his tongue probing for the missing molar. 'How much more might one want back a phantom friend, or even one's sister?' He took her to stay with him in the country after an operation in April.

Her London friends fielded a flood of cards, letters and phone calls from people in France and America who didn't know where to find her. There was a tidal wave of flowers. Bill Coldstream sent a basket of pinks and bluebells, striped lilies, roses, carnations, snapdragons and sweet peas, looped and laced with ribbon ('It's like a great hair-style,' said Amy). Sonia returned to hospital in July. Once again she confided in nobody. Her friends had to piece information together as best they could. She had paid a last visit to Stephen Spender, himself in hospital with both legs in plaster that spring. 'Sonia arrived with armfuls of flowers and a stream of funny stories, it was dazzling,' said Natasha: 'She was very gentle and affectionate, and never said a word about the operation she herself was facing next day.'

The Spenders invited her to stay. So did the Massons. Mary McCarthy sent a long, fond, gossipy letter, begging her to come to Maine for the summer. Francis Bacon's French dealer, Claude Bernard, offered his house and staff. But, when Sonia left hospital in August she could only go as far as Blake's Hotel in South Kensington. The vice-president of Harcourt Brace in New York wrote quoting his chief gunner's mate's morning greeting in wartime:

ME: *Morning, Guns. How's it going?*
GUNS: *Stinking, sir. It's a stinking situation.*

By this time Sonia was back in hospital. 'The garden is missing you,' wrote Michel Leiris, who came himself with Picasso's step-daughter, Catherine Hutin, to say goodbye in November. Michael Pitt-Rivers wrote gravely and gently: 'I can only wish you well and send my love and say that if in any way I can be of help or comfort, you have only to send me a message . . . I am so glad you have such good

friends.' MY NAME IS SONIA, ran a card written in shaky
capital letters from André Masson's little grand-daughter:
YOUR NAME IS SONIA. I KISS YOU SONIA.

She had said she would live to settle the lawsuit and see
the publication of the biography. She did both on Monday
and Tuesday, November 24 and 25, 1980. By Wednesday,
when I visited her in hospital, her reason had clouded over.
Orwell was on her mind but she could no longer talk about
him clearly. She died two weeks later, having paid over
all she had in order to regain control of George Orwell
Productions, which was dissolved under the terms of the
legal settlement. It meant she could leave the copyrights,
and everything else derived from Orwell, back to his
adopted son. She died penniless. Francis Bacon paid her
outstanding hotel bills, and her lawyer warned me not to
count on there being enough left in the estate to cover the
cost of her funeral.

I chose the passage from Ecclesiastes about the breaking
of the golden bowl for her godson, Tom Gross, to read as
the funeral lesson. Afterwards Anthony Powell told me he
had read the same sinister lament at Orwell's funeral thirty
years before. Neither George nor Sonia can have had the
faintest inkling that the charge he laid upon her – or rather
the wilful Orwellian obstinacy with which she tried to carry
it out – would eventually kill her.

In just over twenty years since she died, Sonia's reputation has been systematically blackened. Orwell's subsequent biographers have taken their tone from Crick, who
saw her as greedy and unscrupulous. 'I felt so strongly that
Sonia made no charitable use of the large estate, and that
her high living was so out of character with George Orwell

who would almost certainly have been free with support for poor writers, shaky projects and small big causes, that I quietly set up a small trust . . .' he wrote in *The Times Literary Supplement*. Posterity has reconstructed the Widow Orwell as a cold, calculating gold-digger who shortchanged her husband by marrying him for money, squandering his fortune, exploiting his name and copyrights. Neither refutation nor remonstrance has so far stemmed the tide of venom that pursued her into and beyond the grave.

The posthumous vendetta so distressed Michel Leiris that in 1987 he published a memorial essay, '*Chevauchées d'antan*', dedicating it to Francis Bacon, and taking his central image from that last motoring holiday with Sonia in Brittany. The party had stopped at Comper, supposed birthplace of the Arthurian sorceress Viviane, to visit the forest of Paimpont ('a prosaic name for the remnants of the legendary forest of Brocéliande'), and a pond called the Fairies' Mirror associated with Morgan le Fay. Leiris describes hurrying after Sonia as she rushed ahead through the forest with long strides and hair flying in search of Merlin's Fountain where, according to the tourist hand-outs, the old wizard once called up hurricanes. The fountain turned out to be such a miserable mud puddle that the two of them almost burst out laughing.

But they came back next day, drawn by the poetic power of the place – 'or rather by the power of the old romances invested in it by our imagination' – to find a gang of bikers revving their engines among the trees on the far side of the water, looking in their shiny coloured helmets astride their snorting, bucking chargers like a troop of latterday knights gathered to pay homage to a modern Viviane or Morgan le

Sonia walking with Zette and Michel Leiris
in the early years of their long friendship

Fay. Leiris was haunted by this strange image of Sonia and
the bikers, 'one of the most characteristic of my memories
of the woman whose absence leaves an emptiness that her
old friends find themselves confronting almost daily in its
sad finality'.

No one has conjured up so vividly the brave and generous
spirit her friends loved in spite of perversity and pertur-
bation. Sonia never lost the magical radiance that made
Orwell believe marriage to her would cure him of terminal

TB. Like Orwell himself at the end, Sonia in the last months of her life could still summon sparks of the old magic for the friends who trooped through the tiny hotel room where she lay, propped on pillows, surrounded by flowers and shaded by a dim pink lamp, looking, as Mary McCarthy said, like all the Reynoldses and the Romneys in London's Wallace collection rolled into one.

Acknowledgements and Sources

My principal source has been Sonia's friends, with whom I have talked at length in the twenty years since her death, chief among them her professional colleague Ian Angus, her literary agent the late Mark Hamilton, and Anne Dunn Moynihan, all of whom responded with unfailing patience, generosity and support. I am immensely grateful to Vanessa Parker and Simon Brett; to John Craxton, David Plante, Lady Violet Powell, Lady Spender, Elisabeth Vinaver and Diana Witherby; to M. & Mme Aldo Crommelynck, James Lord, Jean-Yves Moch, Françoise Pitt-Rivers, Georges Vinaver, André and Sybille Zavriew in Paris; and to Sonia's many other friends whose contributions are listed below. My best thanks for help and advice go to Peter Davison, Gill Furlong of the Orwell Archive, Suzi Gablik, William Hamilton of A. M: Heath, Bruce Hunter of David Higham Associates, Rachel Ingalls, Daniel Moynihan, Mrs B. K. George-Perutz of Herbert Smith & Co., T. G. Rosenthal, Philip Stokes and Erica Wagner. My handlers at Hamish Hamilton – Simon Prosser, Juliette Mitchell and Graínne Kelly – could not have been better.

The bulk of Sonia's papers are in the George Orwell Archive at University College, London. Apart from these, and from her letters to me, my main unpublished sources have been her letters to William Coldstream, now in the Tate Archive, and to Michel Leiris in Paris, together with the legal and personal correspondence, documents and papers retrieved by Anne Dunn Moynihan from Sonia's Paris flat, which I have called for convenience the Moynihan Papers. All translations from the French are mine. Where sources are not given in the text, written quotations come from papers in the Orwell Archive, and oral quotations from conversations with me.

Lastly I would like to thank Drue Heinz with the trustees and staff of Hawthornden Castle for the month in which I wrote the better part of this book.

Abbreviations

GO = George Orwell; GOA = George Orwell Archive, University College, London; IA = Ian Angus; JD = Bibliothèque littéraire Jacques Doucet, Paris; MP = Moynihan Papers; SO = Sonia Orwell [or Brownell, or Pitt-Rivers].

Preface

SO's account of her predicament from a letter to Diana Witherby, 14.12.79, kindly shown me by the recipient. The standard account of SO was corrected principally by IA, letter to ed., *The Times Literary Supplement*, 18.10.91; by Anne Dunn, Mark Hamilton and the author, letters to ed., *ibid.*, 25.10.91; by Francis Wyndham, letter to ed., *London Review of Books*, 7.11.91, and by IA, *ibid.*, 26.11.98; by Deirdre Levi, letter to ed., *Spectator*, 11.11.00; and by the author in 'A Victim of her own Loyalty', *Daily Telegraph*, 10.12.91.

Part One. *The First Drop of the Monsoon*

Binnings, Brownells and Dixons

Information, family papers and albums kindly supplied by
Vanessa Parker and Simon Brett. Copies of birth, marriage
and death certificates in India and the UK from the General
Register Office, supplied by IA, who also consulted registers
of Bengal Burials and Baptisms in the India Office Library;
and reports of Brownell's death in *The Statesman and Friend
of India*, 31.12.18, and *The Englishman*, Calcutta, 1.1.19. I am
grateful to Nilima Dutta, Bunny Gupta and Jaya Chaliha for
consulting the Land Assessment registers, Calcutta Municipal Corporation Office, and the registers of St Thomas's
church, Middleton Row, in Calcutta.

Convent of the Sacred Heart, Roehampton

'Man is a Builder' by Sonia Brownell in the *Roehampton
Association Report*, September 1935; information from Sister
M. Coke, Provincial Archivist, Society of the Sacred Heart,
forwarded by Simon Brett; letter to SO from A. White in
GOA; David Plante's comments from his unpublished ts,
'Sonia Orwell', 1991. Quotations from SO come from her
reviews of *Les Amitiés particulières* by Roger Peyrefitte in
Horizon, July 1946, and *Memoirs of a Dutiful Daughter* by S.
de Beauvoir, *London Magazine*, vol. 6, no. 11, Nov. 1959.

Neuchâtel Drowning

Reported in the London *Evening News*, 22.5.36, and *The Times*, 23.5.36, both supplied by IA. SO's review of Moravia's *Paradise and Other Stories* in *Europa Magazine*, no. 6, Jan./ Feb. 1972.

Eugene Vinaver

Letter to SO from Eugene Vinaver in GOA; information from Mrs Elisabeth Vinaver and from Georges Vinaver; 'Eugene Vinaver. Some Recollections' by Elisabeth Vinaver in *The Winawer Saga*, ed. H. M. Winawer, London, 1994; Eugene Vinaver, *The Works of Sir Thomas Malory*, OUP, 1947; letter from SO to B. K. Perutz, 10.10.78, in MP. I am also grateful to Barbara Everett, Dr Kathleen Manville of the *New DNB*, and Philip E. Bennett of the University of Edinburgh.

Euston Road School

Notes of conversations with W. Coldstream and L. Gowing from IA, and see below.

Part Two. The Euston Road Venus

Coldstream & Euston Road School

Information from IA, Olivier Bell, John Craxton, Anne Dunn and Bruce Laughton, SO's ms notes, her letters from W. Coldstream and S. Spender, and her *Horizon* proposal in

GOA; SO's letters to Coldstream in the Tate Gallery Archive, London; IA's notes of conversations with W. Coldstream and L. Gowing; 'The Euston Road Group' by SO in *Horizon*, May 1941; Francis Bacon's comments in *Difficult Women. A Memoir of Three* by David Plante, London, 1983. Further information from *The Paintings of William Coldstream 1908–1987*, eds. Laurence Gowing and David Sylvester, Tate Gallery, 1990; *The Euston Road School* by Bruce Laughton, London, 1986; and *The Affectionate Eye. The Life of Claude Rogers* by Jenny Pery, London, 1995. I have not succeeded in locating the Pasmore portrait, which hung in SO's flat in Percy Street.

Connolly, Watson and Horizon

Information from John Craxton, Anne Dunn, James Lord, Lady Violet Powell, Lady Spender and Diana Witherby; letters to SO from Watson and Connolly (including 'The Id Never Sleeps') in GOA; Connolly's job offer reported by SO to W. Coldstream, 14.11.40,. Tate Archive; letter to SO from Angus Wilson, 8.8.80, in MP; 'The Vamp of the Literati' by John Calder, *Scotsman*, 26.10.91, corrected in Stephen Spender to IA, 6.3.93, GOA. Further information from *Cyril Connolly. A Nostalgic Life* by Clive Fisher, London, 1995; *Cyril Connolly. A Life* by Jeremy Lewis, London, 1997; *Friends of Promise: Cyril Connolly and the World of* Horizon by Michael Shelden, London, 1989; introduction to *The Golden Horizon* by C. Connolly, London, 1953; *A Writer's Notebook* by Anthony Powell, London, 2000; *Journals 1939–83* by Stephen Spender, London, 1985; *Self Portrait with Friends. The Selected Diaries of Cecil Beaton*, ed. R. Buckle,

London, 1979; *Paris after the Liberation* by Antony Beevor and Artemis Cooper, London, 1994; *Tears Before Bedtime* by Barbara Skelton, London, 1987.

Penguin New Writing

Information from *I Am My Brother* by John Lehmann, London, 1960; and *John Lehmann. A Pagan Adventure* by Adrian Wright, London, 1998.

Orwell

Information from IA, Olivier Bell, Celia Goodman, the late Anthony Powell and Lady Violet Powell.

Part Three: The Girl from the Fiction Department

Paris and Merleau-Ponty

Information from IA, M. and Mme Crommelynck, Anne Dunn, Jean-Yves Moch, Janetta Parladé, the late David Sylvester, Diana Witherby, André and Sybille Zavriew; letters to SO from Merleau-Ponty, her comments on him in notebook, and in correspondence with Alfred Métraux, all in GOA; letters from W. Hansen to SO supplied by IA; GO to SO in *The Collected Essays, Journalism and Letters of George Orwell*, ed. Sonia Orwell and Ian Angus, London, 1968, vol. iv. Further information from *The Golden Horizon* by Cyril Connolly, *op. cit.*; 'Les Chevauchées d'antan' by Michel Leiris, *L'Ire des vents*, nos. 15–16, Spring 1987; Spender's *Journals*, *op. cit.*; *The Gilded Gutter Life of Francis Bacon* by Daniel Farson,

London, 1994; *Paris after the Liberation* by Antony Beevor and Artemis Cooper, *op. cit.*; *Simone de Beauvoir. The Woman and her Work* by Margaret Crosland, London, 1992; *Memoirs of a Dutiful Daughter* by Simone de Beauvoir, London, 1958.

SO's comments from:

her review of *Le Sang des autres* by S. de Beauvoir in *Horizon*, June 1946; 'Paris, Spring, 1960' in *The Twentieth Century*, April 1960; reviews of 5 French novels in *London Magazine*, Aug. 1960, *Memoirs of a Dutiful Daughter* by S. de Beauvoir in *London Magazine*, Nov. 1959, and *Aurélien* by Louis Aragon in *Horizon*, Nov. 1945.

Orwell's Marriage to SO, Death and Testament

Information from IA, Jill Balcon, Anne Dunn, the late Lady Violet Powell and Anthony Powell, the late Vera Russell, and Lady Spender; GO's letter to SO, and his Gandhi review in his *Collected Essays*, *op. cit.*, vol. iv; SO's comments on a blank page of one of GO's notebooks, GOA; letter from IA to Michael Shelden, 23.1.22; letter from A. Koestler to GO, 24.9.49, in *The Complete Works of George Orwell*, ed. Peter Davison, assisted by Ian Angus and Sheila Davison, London, 1998, vol. 20; for Richard Blair, see GO to Sir Richard Rees, 17.9.49, *ibid.*, vol. 19; for the night of Orwell's death, see letter from Anne Dunn to ed., *The Times Literary Supplement*, 25.10.91; N. Spender's account of SO's grief from conversation with the author, and letter to Michael Shelden, 27.10.92; letter to SO from Jill Balcon, GOA; copy of GO's will supplied by IA (Sir Richard Rees, appointed joint literary executor with SO, left the running of the estate to her); information on setting-up of GOP and GO's financial dispositions in letter from SO to B. K. George-Perutz of Herbert Smith & Co., 10.10.78, SO's statement for *ibid.*, SO's affidavit dated February 1979, J. Harrison's affidavit, and GOP records, all in MP; see also GO to Gwen O'Shaughnessy in *Collected Essays, op. cit.*, vol. iv, *The Complete Works of George Orwell, op. cit.*, vol. 20, Appendices 3 & 7, and 'Orwell: Balancing the Books' by Peter Davison in *The Library*, vol. 16, June 1994.

Further information from *Difficult Women* by David Plante, *op. cit.*; *George Orwell. A Personal Memoir* by T. R. Fyvel, London 1982; *To Keep the Ball Rolling. The Memoirs of Anthony Powell*, vol. i, *Infants of the Spring*, London, 1976, and vol. iii, *Faces in My Time*, London, 1980; 'A Knight of the Woeful Countenance' by Malcolm Muggeridge in *The World of George Orwell*, ed. Miriam Gross, London, 1971; 'Londoner's Diary', *Evening Standard*, 2.3.55.

Paris and London, Weidenfeld, Israel

Information from Anne Dunn, Miriam Gross, James Lord and Jill Balcon; SO's novel outline in notebook, GOA; letters to SO from Jane & Paul Bowles, Cyril Connolly, Marguerite Duras, Georges Limbour, Jacques Lacan, M. Merleau-Ponty, Janine Queneau, Georges and Diane Bataille, Graham Sutherland, Ian Fleming and Alfred Métraux in GOA; SO's dispatches in the *Sunday Times*, 2.9.56, 30.9.56 & 4.11.56; SO's letters to Leiris in JD. Further information from *Remembering My Good Friends* by George

Weidenfeld, London, 1994; *Cyril Connolly* by Clive Fisher, *op. cit.*; *Cyril Connolly* by Jeremy Lewis, *op. cit.*; *Marguerite Duras. A Life* by Laure Adler, London, 1998; Spender's *Journals, op. cit.*; *Tears Before Bedtime* by Barbara Skelton, *op. cit.*; *The Fifties* by Edmund Wilson, New York, 1983.

Part Four. A Game of Masks

Pitt-Rivers Marriage

Information from IA, John Craxton, Anne Dunn, Janetta Parladé, Françoise Pitt-Rivers, the late Vera Russell, Natasha Spender and Diana Witherby; SO's letters to Leiris (including anon. review – by John Sturrock – of *Fibrilles, La Règle du jeu vol. 3*, from *The Times Literary Supplement*, 15.6.67) in JD; letters to SO from Julian and Margot Pitt-Rivers, A. J. and Dee Ayer, Alfred Métraux, Marguerite Duras, Mary McCarthy, Michael Dixon & Cyril Connolly in GOA; obituaries of Michael Pitt-Rivers, *Daily Telegraph*, 31.12.99 and *Independent*, 11.1.00, and of Julian Pitt-Rivers, *Independent*, 25.8.01; Lee Miller's photos for a cancelled *Vogue* feature in GOA.

Further information from *Against the Law* by Peter Wildeblood, London, 1955; *The Village that Died for England* by Patrick Wright, London, 1995; *Heterosexual Dictatorship. Male Homosexuality in Postwar Britain* by Patrick Higgins, London, 1996; *Vita* by Victoria Glendinning, London, 1983; *A Gift for Admiration. Further Memoirs* by James Lord, New York, 1998; *Secrets of a Woman's Heart. The Later Life of Ivy Compton-Burnett* by Hilary Spurling, London, 1984; 'Regard vers Alfred Métraux' in *Brisées* by M. Leiris, Paris, 1966.

Godchildren

Information from Thomas and Miriam Gross; letters to author from Deirdre Levi, 4.8.01, and from T. Gross to ed., *Spectator*, 9.12.00.

Paris: Art and Literature

Information from Anne Dunn and James Lord.

London: Ivy Compton-Burnett and Francis Bacon

Letters to SO from Francis Bacon and Francis Wyndham in GOA; *Secrets of a Woman's Heart* by Hilary Spurling, *op. cit.*; *The Gilded Gutter Life of Francis Bacon* by Daniel Farson, *op. cit.*; *Difficult Women* by David Plante, *op. cit.*; *A Father and His Fate* by Ivy Compton-Burnett, London, 1957; *Journal 1922–1989* by Michel Leiris, ed. Jean Jamin, Paris, 1992; *Michel Leiris* by Aliette Armel, Paris, 1997; *Francis Bacon ou la brutalité du fait* by M. Leiris, Paris, 1996; *Zébrages* by M. Leiris, ed. Jean Jamin, Paris, 1992; Bacon's tribute in *L'Ire des vents*, Spring 1981; *The Letters of J. R. Ackerley*, ed. Neville Braybrooke, London, 1975.

Part Five. The Widow Orwell

Orwell's Collected Essays

Information from IA and the late Mark Hamilton; letter to author from IA, 18.9.01; reviews by George Steiner in *New Yorker*, 29.3.69, and by M. Muggeridge in *Esquire*, March

1969; letters to SO from Richard Ellmann and M. Duras in GOA; letter from SO to IA, 5.5.96; letters from Mark Hamilton to ed., *The Times Literary Supplement*, 25.10.91, and from IA to *ibid.*, 18.10.91. Further information from *Secrets of a Woman's Heart* by Hilary Spurling, *op. cit.*, and *The Road to Nineteen Eighty-Four* by Peter Lewis, London, 1981.

Friends and Enemies

Information from IA, Miriam Gross and Simon Brett; letters to SO from 'Jules', Jessica Mitford, Iris Murdoch, David Sylvester and Francis Wyndham, GOA; 'Sonia Orwell' by David Plante, *op. cit.*; letters to M. Leiris from SO in JD. Further information from *Angus Wilson* by Margaret Drabble, London, 1995; *Jean Rhys* by Carole Angier, London, 1990; *Stet* by Diana Athill, London, 2000; and *Difficult Women* by David Plante, *op. cit.*

Jack Harrison and George Orwell Productions

Information from the late Mark Hamilton and William Hamilton of A. M. Heath, B. K. Perutz of Herbert Smith & Co., T. G. Rosenthal of Secker & Warburg, Simon Brett and Vanessa Parker; letters from SO to Richard Blair, 2.1.79, and to B. K. Perutz, 10.9.78, SO's statement and affidavit, Feb. 1979, GOP records and correspondence, and J. Harrison's affidavit, all in MP; letter from J. Harrison to Eleanor Blair, 16.11.66, GOA; letters from SO to D. Witherby, 14.12.79 & 10.1.80, in the possession of the recipient; Orwell's sales figures and royalty income from Penguin Books archive, A. M. Heath archive, *All Authors Are Equal* by F. Warburg, London, 1973, *The Politics of Literary Reputation. The Making and Claiming of 'Saint' George Orwell* by John Rodden, Oxford, 1989, and 'Xenophobia Rules – *Geht Das?*' by T. G. Rosenthal, *The Author*, Autumn 1989.

SO's Parisian Exile

Information from Anne Dunn, J-Y. Moch and James Lord; letter from SO to M. Leiris in JD.

Last Return to London

Information from Anne Dunn, Miriam Gross and Natasha Spender; letters to SO from Claude Bernard, Michael Dixon, M. Leiris, André, Rose and Sonia Masson, Mary McCarthy, Julian P. Muller of Harcourt Brace, and M. Pitt-Rivers in MP. Probate on SO's will, initially sworn at £289,109 in 1981, was resworn in 1982 at £75,000, which was swallowed up by legal fees. Bernard Crick, letter to ed., *The Times Literary Supplement*, 1.11.91; 'Les Chevauchées d'antan' by Michel Leiris, *op. cit.*; Mary McCarthy's text read at SO's memorial meeting, Authors Club, London, 10.2.81.

Picture Acknowledgements

Frontispiece – Private Collection/© Succession Picasso/ DACS 2002

Part One

opener – Private Collection
p. 5 – Private Collection
p. 5 – Private Collection
p. 5 – Private Collection
p. 6 – Private Collection
p. 8 – Private Collection
p. 8 – Private Collection
p. 9 – Private Collection
p. 11 – Private Collection
p. 17 – Photograph by Dorothy Wilding. Camera Press
p. 19 – Photograph by Catherine Bell. Private Collection
p. 26 – Private Collection/© All Rights Reserved

Part II

opener – © Courtesy of the artist's estate/Bridgeman Art Library
p. 33 – Private Collection
p. 35 – © British Museum

p. 39 – © Courtesy of the artist's estate / Bridgeman Art Library

p. 44 – Private Collection

p. 46 – Private Collection

p. 50 – Private Collection © the artist

p. 55 – Private Collection / © All Rights Reserved

p. 58 – © All Rights Reserved

p. 60 – © Tate, London 2002

p. 66 – Mr Vernon Richards / The George Orwell Archive, University College, London

Part Three

opener – The George Orwell Archive, University College, London

p. 75 – © Lipnitzki-Viollet

p. 77 – © Bettmann / CORBIS

p. 79 – © Lapi-Viollet

p. 83 – Private Collection / Bridgeman Art Library © the artist

p. 92 – Mr Vernon Richards / The George Orwell Archive, University College, London

p. 98 – The George Orwell Archive, University College, London

p. 106 – The George Orwell Archive, University College, London

p. 109 – © Lipnitzki-Viollet

Part Four

opener – The George Orwell Archive, University College, London

p. 118 – Private Collection © Lee Miller Archive, Chiddingly, England

p. 120 – *Guardian*/E. Hamilton West

p. 125 – Private Collection

p. 127 – © Foundation Trust. Courtesy Private Collection, London

p. 133 – Photograph by Loomis Dean. © Rex/TimePix/Loomis Dean

p. 136 – Photograph by John Vere Brown. © All Rights Reserved)

p. 137 – Photo by Peter Stark. © Peter Stark/Estate of Francis Bacon. Collection Hugh Lane Municipal Gallery of Modern Art, Dublin

p. 139 – Photograph by Suzi Gablik. © Suzi Gablik

p. 140 – Centre Pompidou-MNAM-OCI, Paris © Photo CNAC/MNAM Dist. RMN © The Estate of Francis Bacon 2002/All Rights Reserved. DACS

Part Five

opener – © All Rights Reserved

p. 147 – Private Collection

p. 157 – Private Collection

p. 160 – Photograph by Fay Godwin. © Fay Godwin/Network

p. 170 – Private Collection

p. 177 – © Lee Miller Archive, Chiddingly, England

Every effort has been made to contact all copyright holders. The publishers will be glad to correct in future editions any error or omission brought to their attention.